SIMPLY LIVE IT UP

Brief Solutions

SIMPLY LIVE IT UP

SIMPLY LIVE IT UP

Brief Solutions

TERI-E BELF

CHARLOTTE WARD

Purposeful Press / Bethesda, Maryland

7106 SAUNDERS COURT
BETHESDA, MD 20817
301-365-8112
FAX 301-983-3980

The trademarked name PhotoReading™ and registered names Success Unlimited Network® and The Information-Age Learning Process® appear throughout this book. Although the trademark and registry symbols do not appear with each of the above names, the Publishers state that the names are used only for editorial purposes with no intention of infringing on those marks. "PhotoReading" is a registered service mark of Learning Strategies Corporation, Minneapolis, Minnesota.

Printed in the United States of America by CLB Printing Co., Kensington, MD 20895 on acid-free paper .
Pictographs© by Teri-E Belf
Computer design by Fred Ward; Julia-Set Fractal cover© Fred Ward

Typefaces: Adobe Palatino and Bernhard BTModern

Library of Congress Cataloging-in-Publication Data

Belf, Teri-E, 1946—.
    Simply live it up: brief solutions / Teri-E Belf and Charlotte Ward.

        Bibliography.
        Includes index.
        1. Self-Development.
        2. New-Age Movement.
        3. Learning.
        4. Reading.
        5. Neuro-Linguistic Programming.
    I. Ward, Charlotte, 1937—.   II. Title.   III. Title: Simply live it up: brief solutions

ISBN 0-9646842-0-9   CIP 95-069765

Dedication

To Gussie, my 86-year-young father, who has patiently read drafts and reread and reread. He claims lack of understanding, yet that does not deter his excellent editing, creative language transformations, and beaming accolades coming from the inner depths of his unconditionally loving soul. Gussie serves as my #1 inspiration.

To Fred, my husband, for continual assistance and masterful computer insight. He always sets aside his own work to listen, guide, instruct, and assist me. We have spent many happy hours shaping words to concepts. Our four dear children, Kim, Christopher, Lolly, and David have let me participate in their lives; how else might I have so profoundly learned love, curiosity, and wonder.

40 BRIEF SOLUTIONS

CONTENTS

ACKNOWLEDGMENTS

Teri-E Belf

My husband, Phil, for his consistent stream of encouragement, curiosity, and love.

When the student is ready, the teacher appears. My greatest teacher, my son Kim Allen Williams, continually inspires me to live in the moment—the ultimate brief and perennial solution. My transformation spirals UPWARD whenever I spend time with Kim. He serves as a powerful mirror for my gifts and learning. I feel blessed to have Kim to carry on my purpose, far better than any book could ever do.

Although my Momuschka no longer lives, she would have been so proud—she always was no matter what I did. My family, Jackie, David, Todd, and Kate, Lila, friends, Sharon Hardy, colleagues, mentors, especially Dr. Lucy Zabarenko and Julie Schniewind, SUN network, and clients have shaped me. Without them, I could not SIMPLY LIVE IT UP.

The brief solutions identified as The Results and Well-Being Games, and The Guidelines for Winning are the ingenious creations of Results Unlimited, a British firm that certified me to do Success Coaching. To Jinny Ditzler, Graham Alexander, Ben Cannon, and my coach, Sally Hedges, I thank you for generously allowing me to share these poignant solutions.

The concepts and processes in Chapter 8, "What To Do With Broken Umbrellas," combines material I have developed over 20 years of productivity consulting, as well as pieces from the Managing Accelerated Performance (MAP) Program, developed by Productivity Development Group in the 1980s. Thank you, David Allen and Russell Bishop for crystallizing my applications.

I gifted myself with the openness to partner with one very brilliant soul, Charlotte Ward. If you ever want to have fun writing a book, call Charlotte. I am also extremely grateful to a pure gem, Fred Ward, for sharing his time, wealth of wisdom about authoring, and photographic brilliance.

A special thank you to Pam Leigh, Ron Edins, John Adams, Harrison Owen, Mark Thurston, Elaine Gagné, and Gordon Shea, for graciously carving out time to review this book and offer insightful comments.

Finally I wish to acknowledge myself for giving myself permission to be stuck and uninspired, atypical states of being for me. As I reach new levels of awareness of life's synchronies and blessings, I remember to thank mySelf for allowing the process to unfold in its right time.

Charlotte Ward

For the years of training, professional counsel, and camaraderie, I am grateful to Ron Klein, who opened to me the doors of Ericksonian hypnosis and Neuro-Linguistic Programming, limen to the human mind and heart.

Paul Scheele, author of *The PhotoReading™ Whole Mind System*, Patricia Danielson, Pete Bissonette, and Lynette Ayres, all with Learning Strategies Corporation, have supported my learning to teach the PhotoReading whole mind system, a challenging and rewarding career; as has Peter Kline, a master teacher whose book and training inspired and encouraged me in the field of accelerative learning. I want also to express appreciation to the numerous students in my reading seminars, who have shared their desires and dreams and have willingly suspended disbelief on the edge of knowledge to learn something great and mysterious about their own capacities and potential. I applaud and thank the myriad people who have recorded their ideas in books, so that each of us has a chance to appreciate the discovered patterns of the universe, without having to start at the beginning every time; we can learn from reading as well as from experience.

Madeline Weiss read, out of long friendship, and thoughtfully contributed, out of her storehouse of knowledge. Shelly Greenburg teaches flexibility, balance, strength, and focus, not only through Yoga but also her insightful friendship. She has wisely guided me to explore the middle ground, though I have a proclivity for beginnings and the far edge. Always and ever over the years Joan Conklin and I have shared our ideas and created our philosophies. I appreciate her steady convictions, wisdom, and ever-present willingness to listen.

I owe a debt to my several friends from the extraordinary and unique organization, The Professional Speakers Club of Toastmasters, International. For seven years they listened to my ideas with a rare balance of wit and wisdom; in the process, I sharpened skills in critical thinking and storytelling. To this day, Jill Davis, with a friend's love and an analyst's judgment, patiently weighs every idea I launch and edits precisely and sensitively.

Another alliance forged out of Toastmasters is this work with Teri-E Belf, who delights me with balance between left brain organization and right brain creativity. Long ago I signed on for her to coach me privately in life management. This collaboration proves the success of her strategies.

FOREWORD

The book is extremely well organized. As a reader, I can get anywhere in it I want extremely quickly, and I can always know where I am and what to expect. I've encountered few, if any other books, that handle this so well. That makes it flexible to my needs. Regardless of my background or degree of "counter-exemplardom," I can derive from it easily what I want and need.

You, too, will find new attractions in those previously avoided little corners of impossibility in your life, which you can open up to discover the secret gardens you've forbidden yourself from entering. This book will help you do that.

For example, I had made a contract with myself some years ago never again to buy a piece of furniture that I had to assemble myself. Last week I discovered that if I unpacked that particular limitation, I might both feel better about myself and have to spend less money because I could now unpack a box and make something of my own from what I found there. So I bought three bookshelves and slapped them together with the industry of all Seven Dwarfs working in concert—and I whistled while I Plurked.

What Teri-E and Charlotte have done is to create a book that can be used equally well by many different types of readers with many different backgrounds. You can read this book in five minutes, or you can spend ten years studying it. Perhaps, you will want to do both. And, if you don't happen to like the exercises they've given you, you can use the principles they've expounded on here to make up your own. In fact, it's okay to use this book any way you want, so long as you're using it to change your own life.

The delightful aspect of its organization is that you can start anywhere you want in the book. What I would suggest is that after you've examined the full scope, you find the part that speaks to your current state most eloquently and here begin your work.

Or, if you can free yourself up from the Puritan Work Ethic to have a little fun, try some Plurking with the Plurking Chapter.

The secret of success in any enterprise of self-renewal is to get some change in your life (even one Action Step) as quickly as possible. The energy you'll get from that change will fuel further changes, until finally you'll be ready to take on "the whole thing."

The people whose job security has suddenly gone with the wind so that they have awakened to find they're not in Kansas anymore should read this book and put it to use.

If I were the Secretary of State or the CEO of IBM, I'd buy this book and immediately ship copies to everyone in my organization. I'd realize that the puny investment I'd be making in so many copies of this book would be buying me a huge competitive edge. I'd want to know that everyone was committed to making their lives work as best they could, so they would also make my organization work with the same wholehearted vigor and incorruptible intelligence they had been giving to coaching the Little League team, organizing their garage sale, or conducting a discussion at the family dinner table.

Fads come and go, but there's something about what's at stake here that has been in fashion for the last fifteen billion years (or—as the Hubble has recently suggested to us—perhaps only the last eight billion). Either way, you'll find that complexity is built up from individual units of matter and energy, creating new and wonderful relationships in a holographic context.

Your brain is probably made up of as many independent thinkers, all working together, as New York City would be if all the people in it knew how to pitch in together on the joyful enterprise of making things work. The next time you catch yourself in the throes of a bad habit that's doing you in, give some thought to converting the part of yourself that's powering that bad habit to the central vision of the whole population of selves that make up you, using the tools you'll find in these pages.

This book is your survival kit for living in an age when things are falling apart and the center cannot hold. Robert Greenleaf's notion of the Servant as Leader tells us that anyone anywhere in the system can help organize things to a new level, and *that, obviously, points the finger at you.* If things aren't working in your world, then reorganize whatever parts of your life you need to so that they do work. Or, better yet, Plurk.

Here, then, is a marvelous tool to help you accomplish all this. Like all tools, it's not the only one you'll want to use. It's good because it will help you make more sense out of anything else you may be doing.

So, buy it, read it, use it, and rush out and buy more copies to give to all your friends. That's the best start I can think of to give an additional jump start to the friends who mean the most to you.

Peter Kline
South Bend, Indiana

PREFACE

We invite you now to examine your purposes for reading this book. We have designed it for people who place a strong value on personal growth and development and who are ready to... SIMPLY LIVE IT UP.

Each chapter offers extremely practical, down-to-earth, brief "recipes" to integrate spirit and humanness in a productive way, along with accurate transcriptions of Brief Solutions tested and proven successful by thousands of our clients.

We have each contributed chapters expressing our personal expertise, collaborated on many portions, and coedited this text. We have allowed our distinct voices to come forth.

Over the years, we have read volumes of books and collected quotes. We cannot specifically pinpoint which books some of our quotes came from; however, we delight to give credit to the people whose rich words have touched us.

How To Read This Book:

At the beginning of each chapter we state a problem and some preliminary questions so that you can determine whether you want to read the chapter. Because of the holographic nature of this book, you may find yourself skipping certain chapters and reading others. There may be times you zoom through a chapter and times you stop for reflection. Take what you can use and move on. Just as in life, you cannot participate in everything at once, so choose the ideas you value now.

Examples appear in boxes. We have received permission to share client stories or have changed the names and any identifiers to ensure privacy and anonymity for all concerned.

The structure of this book, like the Julia set on our cover, repeats in each chapter. We provide this prototype to orient you:

PROBLEM names your challenges in today's world—things you want to change.

WHAT IF . . . ?

asks you to describe what result you want. Imagine your future already true with this Brief Solution in place. For example:

- I handle transitions flexibly
- I have all the energy I need to do what I want

THEN invites you to enhance your well-being by adding each Brief

Solution to your accomplishments.

SIMPLY gives an overview of the Brief Solution or Brief Solutions presented in the chapter by answering the questions "Who?" and "What?" Brief Solutions simplify the process of getting from here to there with the least expenditure and maximum return of energy and time. Energy helps you experience your life fully, and time makes it possible to have more of your chosen experiences.

LIVE IT addresses the internal and external benefits to you and others who use the Brief Solutions. LIVE IT, answering the questions "Where?" and "When?" implies taking action in the world, living your own life for yourself, without *should's* compelling you to act. We devote this section to the idea of flowing with life and experiencing well-being as an end in itself.

UP refers to perspective. UP answers the question "So what?" or "What is the significance?" Each chapter contains a section on how to bring awareness of the whole into your daily living. We advocate more than living with tunnel vision. We suggest how we fit into "the big picture," expand our horizons, UPlift ourselves, and bring others to experience UPliftment. We have chosen the Mandelbrot Julia set as our icon to symbolize the seamless interface among multilevel existences.

BRIEF SOLUTIONS answers the question "How?" We identify strategies (tools, techniques, thoughts, habits, and beliefs) to help you SIMPLY LIVE IT UP. With these proven techniques, you can take charge of your life to make it clear, purposeful, flexible, and pleasing to you. Greet the day and the night with positive anticipation, meet adversities with perspective, and make contributions that suit you. Above all, remain forever young by establishing a lifetime habit of learning.

We encourage you to adopt an attitude of lightness, the spirit of **Plurking** (play while working) before reading this book, while reading this book, and after reading this book.

PICTOGRAPH summarizes the chapter in graphic form.

LIST OF BRIEF SOLUTIONS provides a chapter summary.

ACTION invites you to identify the application of each brief solution to your life and urges you to take the Next Action Step.

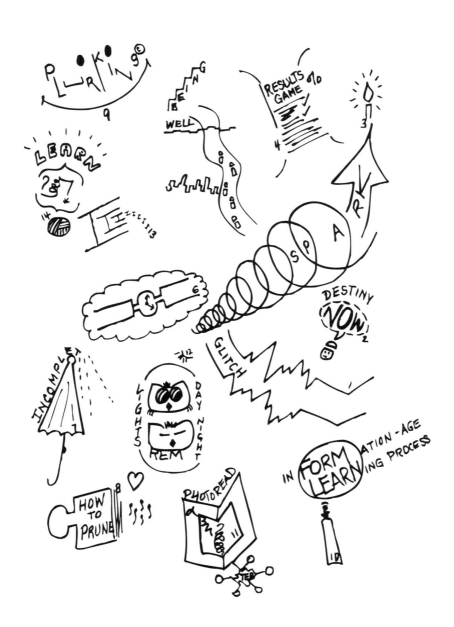

  SIMPLY LIVE IT UP

If you want to use living as the greatest classroom for learning, read Chapter 1, **The Gist of Life is in the Glitches.**

If you want to visualize your results as a way of predisposing yourself to making your goals come true, read Chapter 2, **Design Your Own Destiny.**

If you want to wake UP every morning focused on living purposefully, read Chapter 3, **Re-Energize Your Vital Spark.**

If you want to use a simple mechanism for monitoring daily progress toward your dreams, read Chapter 4, **The Results Game: A Way to Order.**

If you want to "be" life as well as "do" life, read Chapter 5, **The Well-Being Game.**

If you want time as an ally so you can experience self-healing and balance, read Chapter 6, **It's About Time.**

If you want to simplify your life and spring clean the unnecessaries that clutter your physical and mental space, read Chapter 7, **What To Do with Broken Umbrellas.**

If you want to let go of people who no longer support you so you can have more room for family, new friends, and yourSelf, read Chapter 8, **Prune Your People Inventory.**

If you want to play at anything that feels like work, "plurk" with Chapter 9, **Plurking.**

If you want to stay nimble in the Information Age, read Chapter 10, **The Information-Age Learning Process.**

If you want to apply The Information-Age Learning Process to reading, read Chapter 11, **The PhotoReading Whole Mind System**.

If you want to expand choice into the dream state and use wisdom from your dream world in your waking life, read Chapter 12, **REM Realm.**

If you want the flexibility to choose from your multilevels of perspective, read Chapter 13, **Identity and the Infinite I.**

If you want receptivity, curiosity, wonder, and creativity as your approach to living, read Chapter 14, **Simply Live It Up.**

SIMPLY LIVE IT UP

CHAPTER 1

THE GIST OF LIFE
IS IN THE GLITCHES

*No matter what your lot in life might be,
build something on it.*
CA Bell *News*

You are required to make mistakes.
Debi Hinton

The illiterate of the future are not those who cannot read or write, but those who cannot learn, unlearn, and relearn.
Alvin Toffler

I took rejection and turned it into direction.
Sally Jesse Raphael

CHAPTER 1

THE GIST OF LIFE
IS IN THE GLITCHES

PROBLEM

I have so many problems and challenges.
My life is difficult, but no pain, no gain.
I feel annoyed and impatient when people make mistakes.

> *Take the U out of mourning and you get a new day.*
> Church sign in Annandale, Virginia

WHAT IF . . . ?

- I created a new perspective that made my life easy
- I consistently asked, "What can I learn here?"— even when my car broke down

THEN. . .

I would enhance my capacity to create what I want. I would experience the fullness of life's events as gifts. I would focus on flow, not flaws. I would learn from glitches.

SIMPLY

This chapter offers an antidote to problems: learning opportunities. The essence of living is learning. These Brief Solutions embrace how to transform life's challenges and difficulties into opportunities for learning and growth. We encourage and support you at every opportunity to engage in some form of personal UPliftment to increase ease and lightness in your life.

LIVE IT

Many people find the benefits of reframing difficulties into joyful opportunities UPlifting.

Experience is what you get when you do not get what you want.
Author Unknown

Opinion is perspective on a piece of the whole.
Author Unknown

*Making mistakes
simply means you are learning faster.*
Weston H. Agor

So what.
Debi Hinton

UP

When you wake UP and realize that problems outside arise inside, you may see the humor of existence. Viewing your own situation from a macro-perspective encourages flexibility, ease, energy, and love to flourish.

BRIEF SOLUTIONS

1. Convert Glitches to Opportunities

What is a Glitch? A glitch snags or redirects plans and expectations. It appears negative, like a quagmire or mishap, leaving us feeling burdened. Some people call glitches *problems, challenges,* or *difficulties*. We can observe many levels of glitches—personal, national, even planetary. Glitches can be in your home, car, or career.

National Glitch

When Anita Hill accused Clarence Thomas of sexual harassment, the country attentively followed the proceedings. A major glitch in the battle of the sexes? Many now view the hearing as an opportunity for raising consciousness about the male-female chasm and gender oppression in the workplace. This glitch offers us the potential on a massive scale for healing generations of wounds between men and women.

Home Glitch

I came home from visiting my son at summer camp to find that a tornado had ripped through my neighborhood. The first tornado ever recorded there had hit a tiny area only two blocks long. A two-hundred-year-old diseased tree grew on my property. Because removal had been estimated as a costly proposition, I had delayed having it cut down. The storm had lifted the tree from its roots, relocating it so that the top of the tree hid my entire yard. I might have been distressed at this state of affairs. A glitch—or an opportunity?

The insurance assessment assumed that my whole yard would need replanting in the spring and paid for the tree removal as well as new shrubs and foliage.

I cut the tree for firewood, (enough wood for four years), and that spring the yard bloomed with fervor. The absence of the tree allowed in light for a bed of enthusiastic flowers.

One need not be grateful for all experiences life gives,
one need be grateful for the learning
coming from these experiences.
Author Unknown

When life closes one door, it opens another.
Author Unknown

Ventis Secundis. Tene Corsum.
(Go with the flow.)
Author Unknown

Trouble is only opportunity in work clothes.
Henry Kaiser

In 1987, two researchers at the Princeton Engineering Anomalies Research Laboratory of Princeton University (physicist Robert G. Jahn and his colleague, clinical psychologist Brenda J. Dunne), found that "through mental concentration alone, human beings are able to affect the way certain kinds of machines operate."

A familiar glitch is when your car breaks down. Perhaps these mechanical vehicles mirror our foibles and faults. My friend Glenn Kikel, an expert in diagnostic automotive repair, midwifed these analogies with me. Rev UP for a battery of health discoveries that may connect us to our vehicular friends.

Car Glitches

STALLING: If your car keeps stalling and you need towing, ask yourself if somewhere in your life you are stalling.

BRAKES: If your car needs brake repair, you may need to slow down and apply brakes to yourself.

WINDSHIELD WIPERS: If your windshield wipers streak and squeak, see what visions you lack or what areas of your life appear foggy and unclear.

SPARK PLUGS: If your spark plugs corrode or improperly ground, you may need to ground yourself or "clean UP" your self-talk/inner dialogue. If the spark weakens, you may need to revitalize your own spark for living.

FAN BELT: If your fan belt slips, you may be slipping, such as forgetting appointments or losing your keys.

TRANSMISSION: If your trans—mission needs oil or gums up or has worn gears, you may need to revisit your personal mission statement to determine where you feel stuck.

CLUTCH: If your clutch slips, you may need to find new ways to connect to your power source. Consider switching your gears to something different.

ALIGNMENT: If your wheels wobble, your tires wear unevenly, and your gas mileage falls, check your body alignment. Otherwise, you may reduce your personal efficiency or wear out.

KNOCKING: If your car knocks, it may be protesting low octane. You may want to examine your diet.

RADIATOR: If your cooling system overheats or leaks, check to see that both you and your car drink enough water.

Time for inspection? How you treat your car is probably how you treat yourself. What can you learn from your car today?

If you're not operating out of the paradigm
of purposefulness, your life will likely be about your
PROBLEMS.
The "matter of greatest consequence" that claims
your attention during the day will likely be the worries.
If you have purpose, these things become
mere situations to take care of so you can get back to
the important work of making your dream come true.
Joyce Chapman
Live Your Dream

Our capacity to learn helps us live on purpose.
Deepak Chopra
Ageless Body, Timeless Mind

What you try to escape follows you.
What you try to follow escapes you.
Author Unknown

Work Glitch

"You're fired!" "I quit!" That fiery brief exchange occurred the day before Thanksgiving, after my boss asked me to do something unprofessional and against my personal ethics. As a single parent with a mortgage to pay, I might easily have reacted bitterly. However, I managed to immediately transform a crisis by asking myself, "What is the learning and growth opportunity for me now?" I moved out of a detrimental work environment and into discovering my courage and skill as an entrepreneur. On that Thanksgiving Day I had a lot to be thankful for.

Career Glitch

After college I wanted to become a guidance counselor. An assistant in the Guidance Department told me that I needed to teach to gain admittance, so I enrolled in a Master of Education program. My teaching advisor lived the Marine Corps officers' credo, that discipline precedes learning.

While practice teaching, I befriended an older student, George. My advisor briefed me that he was a hopeless case, yet I felt the need to establish a caring connection. George hardly spoke. He seemed to live in a imaginary internal world. I discovered that when I asked him to draw his learning, he produced intelligent artistic answers.

My advisor eventually learned that George and I had a unique way of communicating. He scolded me for caring too much about one student. The next day when George came to school, my advisor beat him with a paddle in front of his classmates. Horrified, I fled to the department head, only to be threatened that if I told the news media (because beating was illegal), they would blackball me from ever teaching in the city. I quit the program right before graduation.

Instead I decided to find a job. The Education Research Department needed a summer intern. I qualified. Excited and challenged, I chose to obtain an Education Research degree. Just two months earlier I had never heard of the field. My whole life changed because of a glitch. Retrospectively, it was my blessing.

The premise behind converting glitches to opportunities is that we can control our responses to everything that happens to us. We can choose the interpretation we put on an event. We can use everything for our advancement and upliftment. (*Advancement* here

GLITCH *PLURKSHEET©

Identify three recent glitches

GLITCH 1 _____

_____

What did you learn from this experience?
(Learning can take place at many levels: mind, body, spirit, emotions, knowledge, skills, or attitudes.)

_____

_____

GLITCH 2 _____

_____

What did you learn from this experience?

_____

GLITCH 3 _____

_____

What did you learn from this experience?

_____

_____

What is the connection among the glitches?

What is the connection among the things I learned?

Plurk = play + work

means personal growth, not career advancement). Or, we can perceive problems as negative and risk spiraling down into frustration, cynicism, anger, despair and hopelessness. Our choice.

Identify your last three glitches on the Glitch Plurksheet[©] (*Plurk* means play while working) to discover the learning.

2. Maintain the Learning Posture

The Japanese phrase, *Manabu Shisei O Tamotsu*, translates to "maintain the learning posture." Some Japanese companies place such a high value on learning that they have replaced the coffee break with a learning break. During the learning break, employees may think, read, meditate, or practice anything else that keeps them in the learning posture. As people maintain the learning posture, they deal flexibly with change, the byline of most companies these days.

Do you wonder why many Americans have difficulty adapting to the changing workplace, workforce, and merger/downsizing trends? The typical American company has coffee breaks during which many employees engage in addictions (coffee, cigarettes). Addictions keep people rigid and programmed into bad habits. Learning keeps us flexible at "growing" with the flow.

Use yourself as an experimental playground. LEARN. LEARN. LEARN. Increase your wonder and curiosity. Get into the habit of seeing everything as a learning opportunity.

Do you create your own glitches? Perhaps a combination of glitches and intention creates our destiny.

- When I focused on my state of being, honey bees inhabited my garden.
- When I felt "antsy" (unsettled), armies of ants invaded my kitchen.
- When I felt life was moving too quickly and said I wished it would stop, the next day, I was involved in a car accident, which stopped me. I couldn't move—my car or my body.
- Recently, when I concentrated at being in the flow, I developed an intense case of diarrhea.
- I can easily work four hours without stopping. I need to be reminded to take breaks to maintain my well-being. When Charlotte edited my writing, she added about two hundred commas. At our next meeting, she pointed out that the comma represents a pause—time to take a breath, a necessary break in the flow of reading. I found this coincidence amusing, then remembered that last year, I met a delightful colleague named Comma.

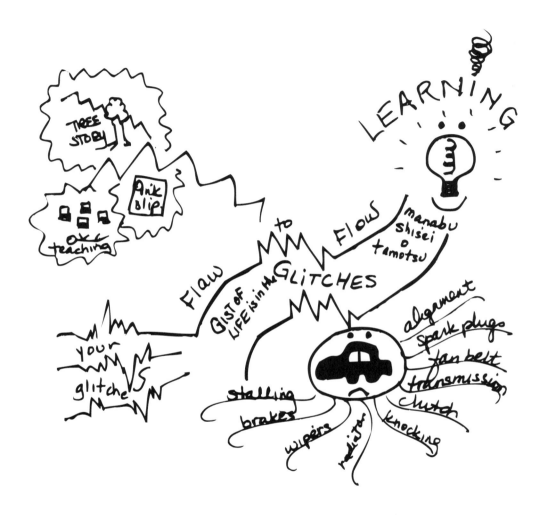

SIMPLY LIVE IT UP

Our brain mechanism, the reticular system, sometimes called the reticular activating system or RAS, alerts us like a homing device. We can put this primitive safety network to positive conscious use to aid learning. We continue to get glitch messages until we pay attention!

3. Flee Flaw; Follow Flow

One way to create glitches is to view experiences through a magnifying glass. Do you know anyone who analyzes, processes, evaluates, and criticizes every move, every feeling, every reaction? Faultfinders beam their reticular system on what is wrong. They carry magnifying glasses to enlarge flaws and imperfections instead of welcoming mistakes as markers for learning.

When I feel impatient with my husband, I view my own impatience. I only recognize his impatience because of my own. When I feel angry toward the airlines for delaying my flights, I hold UP the mirror to look into my own anger.

To transform from a flaw-finder to a flow-finder, throw out the magnifying glass and pick UP the mirror. We all serve as mirrors for each other. What I see in you is a reflection of me. Noticing you does not necessarily teach me about you but rather about myself.

LIST OF BRIEF SOLUTIONS for Chapter 1

1. Convert Glitches to Opportunities: Learn from Your Car Problems
2. Maintain the Learning Posture
3. Flee Flaw; Follow Flow

ACTION

How do I intend to apply these solutions to my life to get the results I want?

What Next Action Step do I plan to take?

Once you develop the habit of maintaining the learning posture and transforming glitches to opportunities, you are ready to rehearse success. Chapter 2 tells how to **Design Your Own Destiny**.

CHAPTER 2

DESIGN
YOUR OWN DESTINY

*Belief is the formalization of meaning fossilized. It
becomes rock on which a personal fortress can be built.
However, a shelter constructed out of ever-shifting
understanding becomes a magic carpet,
leaving the earthbound behind.*
Nelson Zink
The Structure of Delight

To some extent, reality is an agreed-upon fiction.
Diane Ackerman
The History of the Natural Senses

Perfection is not a reality but an intention.
Reinhold Niebuhr
Nature and Destiny of Man

Once we make our decision,
all things will come to us.
Auspicious signs are not a superstition,
but a confirmation. They are a response.
Deng Ming-Dao
Tao

CHAPTER 2

DESIGN YOUR OWN DESTINY

PROBLEM

Other people do it better than I. I'm just a beginner, and I'm scared.
What if I fail? What if I never do it perfectly?
What if they don't like it?
I need to grow into this job.
Is there an escape clause?
My problem is facing the future, facing the unknown, facing the fear of failure.

> *You can pretend anything until you master it.*
> Milton H. Erickson

WHAT IF . . . ?

- I set my sights on something I have always wanted
- I gave my imagination free rein to flesh out my dreams
- I sensed how I interact with others with this skill in place
- I talked to myself only in terms of excellence
- I noticed what lessons I have learned and obstacles I have overcome to get here
- I revelled in my feelings of mastery and memorized them

THEN . . .

I would get an immediate reward. Mastery would be my resource for any challenge. I would assume the understanding, internal voice, and body language as if I had already achieved it. This ploy would coach my body into a self-fulfilling prophecy. Then, when I actually began the new activity, I would already know the ropes.

SIMPLY

This chapter features experiencing the future now. I choose my tomorrow to be the best, lightest, and easiest I can imagine. If I can imagine it, I can LIVE IT.

The paradox of our times:
by the time you know where you ought to go,
it's too late to go there, or, more dramatically,
if you keep on going the way you are,
you will miss the road to the future.
Charles Handy
The Age of Paradox

People who are fearless attract me.
Kevyn Aucoin, Makeup Artist and Author
Los Angeles *Times*, Thursday, January 12, 1995

We are outcomes waiting to happen.
Robert Stevens Tennyson

Only use the past as resource.
Charlotte Ward

LIVE IT

Experience your future in your imagination, then in real life. Peak performance business people, individuals, and athletes use visualization as one powerful strategy to achieve their goals. Olympic-Gold bobsled driver, Gustav Weder prepared each day by laying out a photographic montage, going into state, and running the course in his imagination—talking out loud, taking each turn in turn.

And Olympic figureskater Brian Boitano related where he went wrong in landing his crucial long program triple axel. He kept pressuring himself, "I have to land this jump," instead of what he usually says, "Leg up, lift, pull in arms fast, turn hard...." Designing your own destiny activates the body-mind into the same neural firing as doing the real thing, with a delightful difference—success from the beginning. Instead of problematic trial and error, you start with positive expectation already in place. Because the path of success looks, sounds, and feels familiar, it invites you to enjoy the acquisition, not as new but as habit, not with fear of failure but with the security and expectancy of success.

> Shirley wanted to learn windsurfing, so she hired a renowned coach, Charles Parry. He instructed her to watch a video, then spend one week visualizing herself in action. What had appeared a difficult challenge turned into a breeze, first time up.

Attaining mastery begins with demystifying it: Masters employ strategies and persistence. The more successfully you assume rapport with the master, the briefer the time to expertise. We learn by doing. To attain mastery, assume the master's physical posture, thinking process, and emotional state—determination, expectation, and macro-perspective. Both pain and pleasure affect learning: pain lets you know what to avoid; pleasure, what to embrace. You can use your imagination to program what you do, think, and feel; expect the best and choose pleasurable learning every day.

UP

Program your lifelong achievements. If UP points to where you want to be, as soon as you imagine yourself getting the results you want, you have already taken a giant step.

BRIEF SOLUTION: Design Your Own Destiny

You have brains in your head
You have feet in your shoes.
You can steer yourself
any direction you choose.
Dr. Seuss
Oh, The Places You'll Go!

Life is shaped as much by the future as by the past.
Mihaly Csikszentmihalyi

Because of necessity, man acquires organs.
So, necessitous one, increase your need.
Rumi
Thirteenth Century Sage

You are what your deep driving desire is;
As your deep driving desire is, so is your will;
As your will is, so is your deed;
As your deed is, so is your destiny.
The Upanishads

1. What Do You *Not* Want? Think of what you do *not* want or what you want to avoid. Project what your future will be like should you continue that behavior over the next year? Over five years?

2. What Do You Want that Will Align You with Your Ideals? Now, separate *do not* from *do,* and leave the problem behind. Delete all negative and equivocal language, such as *don't want, work on, really, should, try, maybe, truly, perhaps, be able to.* Simply finish the sentence that begins *I want...,* and identify the *antithesis*—what you WANT. It may help you to identify exactly what you want by thinking how someone else goes about getting the desired result. Then state that result in a positive sentence and put *I want* at the beginning. Adjust the statement until it pleases you.

3. Pictograph Your Desired Result with at least three colors.

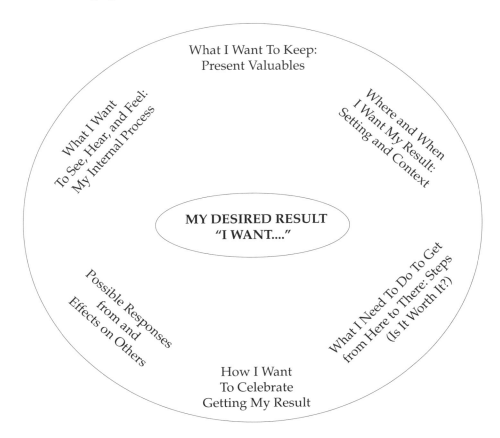

*The voyage of discovery lies not in finding
new landscapes,
but in having new eyes.*
Marcel Proust

Brain Wave States

β Beta level, 14-33 Hertz: fully conscious; external state of action; doing; curiosity and wonder; questioning

α Alpha level, 8-14 Hertz: open or closed eyes; relaxed and alert; enhanced concentration and performance of an activity; awareness of surroundings if asked; inner focus; ideal state for intaking information; routine habits and patterns of the day; floating; daydreaming

θ Theta level, 4-8 Hertz: subliminal; aware of being in state and aware of coming out; recognizable as day or night dreaming; rapid eye movement (REM) sleep; bridge between Alpha and Delta; eyes usually closed; focused within; ideal state to integrate information; state of creativity; parallel number of cycles per second with largo beat of Baroque music; source of *aha*; active mind, inactive body; symbolism

Δ Delta level, .5-4 Hertz: deep sleep; closed eyes; resting body and mind

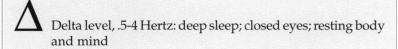

Live in state or lie in state.

On New Years's Eve Jill arrived with the surprise activity to herald the new year. Unloading magazines, large frames, and colored paper onto my dining room table, she also produced glue sticks, scissors, and colored markers. Accompanied by Brahms trios, for the next three hours, we each made a collage of our goals and dreams for the coming year. Like kids in kindergarten, we cut and arranged pictures and text into bright groups around big numbers signifying the year to come. Just as the old year drew to a close, we glued the last of our images to the backing and fitted our dreams into frames to hang over our desks.

Every time I passed my creation, I remembered the fun my friend and I had had; and near the end of that year, I realized I had achieved almost every single pictured wish. For me there is no better way to celebrate than to see what I have accomplished and to pictograph my goals with anticipation.

4. Follow this Script on a Tour of Your Future. Take a self-guided tour, ask a friend to read the script to you, or tape-record it with pauses long enough to mentally perform each step. Where the mind explores, the body knows the way.

Choose a *sitio*, a quiet spot where you can concentrate. Relax into a frame of mind that feels like day dreaming; shift your attention from the outside world to within.

Relax. Let your body melt into a resting position. Relax. Let the space of your mind flow open and boundless.

Now state the result you want, a combination of *do* and *be*. Align your desired result with your ideals, and imagine getting this result in an appropriate scene, or context. In every way, imagine the result you desire in the future already occurring in the present moment. Speak in the present tense, breathing evenly and fully.

In your mind's eye or on an imaginary screen, envision yourself in the context you chose approaching the time when you want to achieve your new result. When your image on the screen reaches the decision point, see that it chooses to do things to get your result. Follow the action

Bonny wanted the result of writing vividly and to the point. After she took the PhotoReading seminar, she came for a private follow-up session. She told me that whenever she used her advanced reading skills, she received A's in her university classes. Still, she worried that she did not use them consistently. I asked her to recall something that might be stopping her. Bonny immediately remembered her reading teacher in fourth grade. Before then, Bonny's parents had home-schooled her on the family boat in the Virgin Islands.

When Bonny began regular school, she placed in the highest reading group. She loved her first day's reading homework so much she couldn't put the book down. The next day in front of her class, instead of commending her, the teacher "yelled" at her for "going ahead." When I asked Bonny if she remembered her teacher's name, her gray eyes widened with the joke, "Mrs. Reid!" Bonny immediately realized that to enjoy stories, she had had to "talk around" Mrs. Reid.

This semester she wants to write a short story expressing her excitement about competition riding. I urged her to detail an event to help me imagine what it was like to clear an obstacle. Pictographing, Bonny fluently related skills and feelings: pausing six paces back to collect rider and horse, advancing, her body taking on tone, and breathing up as she and her horse arc together over the rail. As she jumped in her imagination, Bonny sat forward with curved back, balanced in the saddle. She described the flow of movement succinctly with well-chosen detail, all of which had connected to her central purpose. I felt as if I had just seen her clear the last obstacle for the Blue Ribbon.

Now Bonny has perspective on Mrs. Reid's rules. She writes clearly and vividly, and consistently uses PhotoReading (See Chapter 11).

until your image gets what you want. Fill the scene with whatever you need to make it safe, fun, and personally powerful. Add any resources from the past or actions of a role model to make your best future. Adjust the action until you have the movie or slide show or TV show just the way you want it—from the beginning of the sequence through the decision point to the successful completion. See yourself doing what you want and reaping the rewards. Make the picture appealing. Imbue the future you with any resources you need to complete your result.

When everything in the scene looks the way you want it, step into the screen personality and integrate the feelings of competence and confidence that attend mastery. Now notice your feelings, internal voice, and surroundings. Look along your timeline to the past you; notice the obstacles you have come over, under, around, and through to achieve your present level of success. Enjoy how far you have come after having decided what you wanted. Notice how you interact with others—at home, at work or school, in social situations. Feel the good feelings and memorize them.

From this perspective, create another screen beyond, when you will have enjoyed mastery for perhaps three to five years. How does life look with your chosen result having been a habit for several years? Transport all resources that apply, and when the scene looks just the way you want, step into this picture, and integrate. As a master, how do you interface with the world now, and how does the world look, sound, and feel to you? Hear the voices, feel the feelings of accomplishment and ease, and see what you see from these eyes. Memorize your good feelings. Wrap them around you like a mantle of light.

From this vantage, look back along the timeline past the nearer image to the moment you decided in favor of your result. Notice how far you have come and how comfortable you are with your accomplishment as a foregone conclusion. Notice what obstacles you have overcome to

SIMPLY LIVE IT UP

reach mastery and the rewards you now enjoy.

Gently retrace your journey along your timeline from your future back to your *sitio*. In this present moment, keep with you all the positive feelings, thoughts, and images from your imagined future. These future "memories" belong to you now. You know the way because you have already been there. And during the weeks and months and years to come, you may delightfully surprise yourself by getting your desired results throughout your life.

Keep this future you as a guide. If you wish, thank your imaginative Self for lighting the way. Once again be aware of the room and the world about you and your living potential to manifest results.

BRIEF SOLUTION for Chapter 2: Design your Own Destiny

STEPS
1. What do you *not* want?
2. What do you want that will align you with your ideals?
3. Pictograph your desired result
4. Follow the script on a tour of your future

ACTION

How do I intend to apply this solution to my life to get the results I want?

What Next Action Step do I plan to take?

Transforming glitches into learning adventures and designing your own destiny require focused energy. Learn to tap into your power source, your vital spark, by playing the Go to Purpose Game in your everyday life. The next chapter, **Re-Energize Your Vital Spark**, offers creative Brief Solutions for purposeful living.

CHAPTER 3

RE-ENERGIZE
YOUR VITAL SPARK

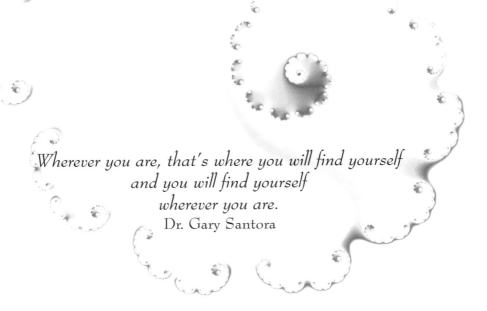

*Wherever you are, that's where you will find yourself
and you will find yourself
wherever you are.*
Dr. Gary Santora

Success is not the result of spontaneous combustion.
You must set yourself on fire.
Reggie Leach

Great power is always produced through
a process of focalizing a specific force
into a confined area.
Uranda

Until you are at home somewhere,
you cannot be at home everywhere.
Mary Catherine Bateson
Peripheral Visions: Learning Along the Way

CHAPTER 3

RE-ENERGIZE YOUR VITAL SPARK

PROBLEM

My life seems to make no sense. It is just a random series of discon-
nected events with me in the middle.
Sometimes I feel bored and lazy.
I become stuck with indecision when I have too many choices.
I feel lonely and distant when I travel and live out of hotel rooms.

Make yourself an efficient spark plug,
igniting the latent energy of those about you.
David Seabury

WHAT IF . . . ?

- I felt as if I were living on my purpose even when I did
  routine things, such as shopping
- I interpreted my physical body messages and used that
  information to steer my daily choices
- I felt "at home" no matter where, even in a hotel room

THEN . . .

I would live purposefully with ease in all areas of my life,
including shopping, selecting a job, and traveling. In a bookstore, in
a closet, on an airplane, or wherever else I went, I would feel free to
be purposeful. When I chose purposefully, I would feel enthusiastic.

SIMPLY

To help you make choices consistent with your life purpose,
we present a potpourri of tips in this chapter to help you **purposefully** 1. notice the physical signs that indicate you are on purpose, 2.
select your next job, 3. shop, 4. feel at home while traveling, and 5.
Plurk in a bookstore or in a closet or on an airplane.
This chapter means more if you already know your life pur-

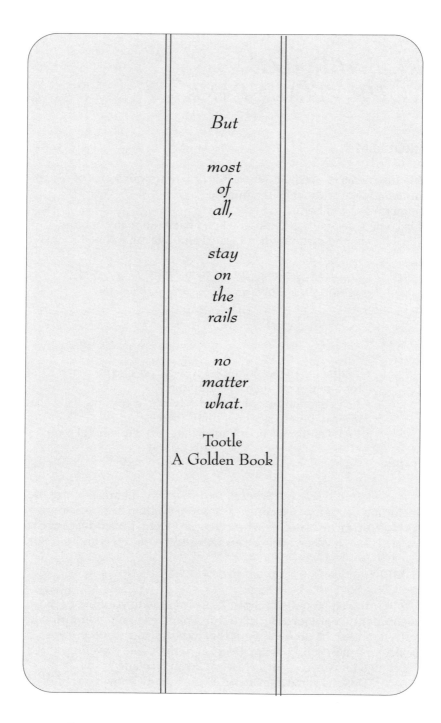

But

most
of
all,

stay
on
the
rails

no
matter
what.

Tootle
A Golden Book

SIMPLY LIVE IT UP

pose. If you do not, contact us. You can make purposeful choices for major life events as well as for daily routine activities. Here you will discover practical ways to live on purpose consistently.

LIVE IT

If you don't know where you are going,
any road will take you there.
Lewis Carroll
Cheshire Cat in *Alice in Wonderland*

Do you know where you are going? Do you know how to stay on the road that consistently brings you the results you want with a true sense of well-being, satisfaction, and fulfillment? Or do you occasionally veer onto the shoulders by mistake, miss the road signs, or get stuck on a dead end street?

When you know your life purpose, you know your personal unique road map. With it you can travel with clarity and direction, if you can interpret what your physical body is telling you. Then you find yourself in the driver's seat of your life, and you can **choose with ease** where to drive, how fast to go, and when to rest.

UP

You have free will to respond to everything that comes to you, including mishaps. You have seen how each glitch has a hidden learning opportunity. If we act purposefully, we can enjoy the richness that attends the multilevels of our awareness and of our universe. Your purpose is your spirit expressed. When you make choices consistent with your purpose, you can SIMPLY LIVE IT UP.

BRIEF SOLUTIONS

1. Carnal Encyclopedia

My purpose in life is to inspire and guide people to take steps toward their dreams. I manifest my purpose by introducing people to the habit of making choices within life's natural progression as they confidently move toward their dreams and live consistently on their life purpose.

Have you had a vague feeling about your purpose for many years yet have not expressed it in exact language? Your choices may have appeared to you more trial and error than purposeful. How do you know whether you make choices consistent with your purpose?

Live Your Purpose

Live   your purpose,
         your passion,
         your place.
Practice
         pleasantly prancing,
Practice
         poignantly producing,
Practice
         powerfully playing,

Persevere with persistent pursuit of the plentiful.
and you will be in the presence of your

PRIZE POSSESSION—

                    purposefulness.

Teri-E Belf

  SIMPLY LIVE IT UP

Your body has that data. You need to know how to interpret it.

Clients have reported many different physical clues to feeling purposeful, ranging from tingling, goose bumps, energy flush, warmth in the area around the heart, fullness in the chest, and lightness. Some people hear words or phrases or ringing in their ears. Your dominant mode of interpreting the world externally may differ from how you sense it internally.

> For years Tamara felt frustrated because she thought her guidance would come by seeing color or wispy shapes. I suggested that she tune into another sense, where she discovered she could easily diagnose purposefulness by listening internally. Now she hears her purpose information in words.

Having an inner knowing or feeling of purpose constitutes a good first step but doesn't complete the process. By writing things down, we bring internal focus on external events. Consistently express your purpose in writing to design your own destiny.

2. The Unannounced Walkabout

Much of our spark ignites or sputters in the workplace. Years ago I had a job with exciting content, intellectually rewarding challenges, and good pay, yet the business environment felt very stressful. The office space was unimaginative, dirty, noisy, and poorly ventilated with windows that could not open. Old posters and outdated calendars faded on the walls, tape and paper littered the area around the copy machine, and people had long since stained and worn the carpeting. My productivity suffered in this environment.

I had focused on the work itself during my initial job interview, but intellectual stimulation and salary were only two pieces in my job criteria puzzle. I had forgotten other values. I also value beauty, aesthetics, art, and a neat, clean, physical space. The environment must support my values for me to experience my inspiration.

After that experience, I invented the **unannounced walkabout** as a job-search strategy. On an unannounced walkabout, you visit a potential place of employment immediately before or right after your interview. If you need a pretense, ask to use the restroom. This walkabout enables you to assess congruence between the company's stated values and the company's reality. During the walkabout, look for clues about the company's values. After the walkabout, determine synergy with yours.

VALUE YOUR VALUES

Select 5-8 Top Values	My Values	COMPANIES Job 1	Job 2	Job 3
Adventure				
Aesthetics				
Affection				
Altruism				
Appearance				
Commitment to goals				
Community				
Control of environment				
Cooperation				
Creativity				
Flexibility				
Friendship				
Good working conditions				
Home life				
Independence				
Integrity				
Leadership				
Mastery/achievement				
Meaningful work				
Money				
Ownership				
Personal growth /development				
Physical health				
Pleasure (enjoyment, fun)				
Privacy (solitude)				
Quality				
Recognition and feedback				
Security				
Service				
Spirituality				
Stability				
Teamwork				
Wisdom				

Consider your key values. Is orderliness important to you? How about ambiance, the feel of a space as you enter it? Do you need a beautiful, creative environment with color, art work, living plants, and natural light to bring out your best work? Must you have state-of-the-art technology? Include these as criteria in your job search.

Rick's strongest values are good working conditions, recognition and feedback, and creativity. During his unannounced walkabout, he noticed these clues: leading-edge computers and other equipment, framed employee awards on the walls, an employee-of-the-month section in the newsletter, available for all to see, and tasteful wall hangings. He preprogrammed his senses for clues that supported his values, and he found a good match.

The unannounced walkabout may be the only way you can obtain valid value information. Human resource recruiters converse about job skills and benefits. They rarely speak about the company's values; often they cannot identify them.

Read an annual report to see if the values are explicitly spelled out in a mission statement or the President's/CEO's message. The walkabout still helps you determine if the values actually exist in the environment.

How do you know what you value? **Your values enable you to make meaningful choices.**

V   • **V**alues represent consistent behavior in several circumstances. Acting once or twice in a particular way does not indicate a value.

A   • You can deduce your values by observing your **A**ctions. Your stated beliefs may say one thing, your actions another. Your actions broadcast what you regard as significant.

L   • Values suggest something you **L**ike.

U   • Each one of us possesses a **U**nique profile of values. It seems easy to relate to someone who has similar values.

E   • Values motivate, propel, and **E**nergize us to action.

Identify your five to eight key values using the list. Then take a walkabout. Applicants often overlook aspects that can make or break their work experience. Clients who have used the walkabout have reported insights and better job selection.

3. Shopping on Purpose

Purpose relates to everyday experiences, even shopping. Among my long list of errands to do before evening, I needed a gift for someone who has everything. Closing my eyes, I asked that the "perfect gift" appear easily and quickly, adding, "I choose to act purposefully for the highest good." The first store I felt compelled to enter had the perfect gift. I expressed gratitude to the powers above, and spent the rest of the shopping day sequencing through silent

He who sets his mat straight....
Confucious

*Purpose serves as a principle
around which to organize our lives.*
Author Unknown

The purpose of life is to live a life of purpose.
Richard Leider

Great minds have purposes, others have wishes.
Washington Irving

SIMPLY LIVE IT UP

moments, purposeful observation, and gratitude. What a day! Even handy parking spaces opened UP. The universe provided.

How often have you been pressed for time when you needed to buy something? Imagine the payoff if you first tuned inside to discover what might help you in this endeavor.

4. Necessary Bag

The biggest complaint I hear from people who travel is that they feel lonely. Why not take home along?

Pack a few objects that represent the feeling of home, such as a favorite knickknack, a photo, a crystal, a letter opener, a memento from a special event. When you enter the hotel room, create a sanctuary with your special objects. By carrying these items with you on your travels, you can transport your home energy with you. With these objects in place, you can easily acclimate to a new room.

The typical travel packing list always includes a cosmetic kit or shaving kit, a toothbrush, deodorant...for your physical needs. How about preparing a necessary bag for your mental/emotional needs—a portable mental care packet? Tuck in these special items too:

> Purpose statement
> Visions and annual goals
> Guidelines for Winning (Chapter 4)
> Results Game (Chapter 4)
> Projects and Next Action Step Lists (Chapter 7)

5. Go to Purpose Game

Play the Go to Purpose Game as often as you like, anywhere, any time, all the time, with anyone, with everyone.

IN A BOOKSTORE

I went into a bookstore with the expressed purpose of finding a perfect quote for one of these chapters. I closed my eyes to state my intent; then I opened my eyes and walked until I felt compelled to stop. My eyes rested on a book, so I picked it UP, and opened it. At that point I trusted that the perfect quote was somewhere on the two pages in front of me. And it was!

IN A CLOSET

If you tend to prepare your clothes the night before, wait! Wake UP tomorrow morning and play the Go to Purpose Game in your clothes closet.

When I know something is right, I get a bing, bing, bing, and a smile gets caught up in my jaw.
Natalie Kalogeraki

Energy creates energy. It is by spending oneself that one becomes rich.
Sarah Bernhardt

Passion doesn't come from business or even a connection with another person. It is a connection to your own life force, the world around you, and the spirit that connects us all.
Jennifer James
Success is the Quality of Your Journey

Begin by focusing on your day. Will you need to dress for business, casual, play, and dressy clothes? Open your closet; close your eyes. Restate your day's purpose. Reach out and select something. Perfect for today, right? For fun, do the same thing with your other hand.

ON AN AIRPLANE

You can engage in purposeful UPlifting connections. Every trip, business and pleasure, provides a rare uninterrupted interlude to visit with a seatmate. True, it may take courage to initiate a conversation and to disclose something about yourself. Take a risk, you may find it worthwhile.

> • *Resourcing:* Everyone offers a database of resources. For months I sought the name of an underground mine in Virginia. By chance (?), I sat next to the National Director of Mines.
>
> • *Marketing:* From Cleveland to Denver I chatted with the president of an insurance company who enrolled in my program before we landed. I closed a contract 35,000 feet in the air.
>
> • *Service:* You gain value by offering to serve. Once I entertained a normally active two-year old boy while his mother took a well-deserved nap. How grateful she was! What fun I had!
>
> • *Networking:* Tapping into my career network brought fortune to a recent Harvard MBA graduate who was seeking business connections in Washington, D.C. He landed several leads.
>
> • *Historical Retracing Assistance:* Have you ever regretted losing contact with colleagues, yet never bothered to do anything about it due to how much time you would need to track them down? I had lost touch with my Pittsburgh colleagues from 23 years ago. Coincidentally (?) I sat next to a Swiss woman who had just completed a six-month internship at the same Pittsburgh clinic. In two hours I got an UPdate on the intervening years.
>
> • *Professional UPdate:* So many of us have books that we expect to get to one day stacked by our bedside. How would you like to meet an author directly and discuss a book firsthand?
>
> • *Listener:* Sometimes I function as a temporary therapist. I recall roleplaying with a gay executive, who practiced "coming out of the closet." Later that month, I counseled a woman in the throes of "picking UP the pieces" after her divorce.
>
> • *News:* Would you like a personal hot line for current events? On one trip, a Christian Science *Monitor* news correspondent just returning from the former Soviet Union shared with me what was "really going on."

SIMPLY LIVE IT UP

You may have many prospects for in-flight experiences where taking the risk can repay the effort. Trust the process, take a purposeful risk, explore your human surroundings. You may find a job, a contract, a date, a publisher, or a new friend. When you take your next flight, arive at your seat and possible opportunities in addition to merely arriving at your destination.

6. A Purposeful Start

How do you start your day? Is your first wake-up thought in the morning "What is the most purposeful thing I am going to do or experience today?"Use the books in our bibliography to help you identify your life purpose. Thinking purposefully reconnects you with your constant, stable, and familiar Self.

In this chapter, we applied purposefulness to daily activities, such as shopping, selecting clothes, and traveling. Play the Go to Purpose Game in other areas, such as leisure, health, friendships, and work. Can you conceive of a life in which you play the Go to Purpose Game every moment? Use your imagination to apply the principle of purposefulness to all you do, and you will start to notice ease, focus, and clarity. Keep your spark ignited.

LIST OF BRIEF SOLUTIONS for Chapter 3

1. Carnal Encyclopedia
2. The Unannounced Walkabout
3. Shopping on Purpose
4. Necessary Bag
5. Go to Purpose Game
6. A Purposeful Start

ACTION

How do I intend to apply these solutions to my life to get the results I want?

What Next Action Step do I plan to take?

Purposeful living keeps your vital spark ignited. What can you focus your energy on? The results you want! Chapter 4 introduces **The Results Game: A Way To Order**, a practical process to effectively focus your energy and create Guidelines for Winning.

SIMPLY LIVE IT UP

CHAPTER 4

THE RESULTS GAME: A WAY TO ORDER

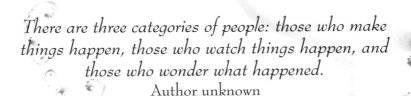

There are three categories of people: those who make things happen, those who watch things happen, and those who wonder what happened.
Author unknown

Life is a game and it comes without instructions.
Ziggy

Learning is the antidote to aging.
Deepak Chopra

CHAPTER 4

THE RESULTS GAME: A WAY TO ORDER

PROBLEM

I don't have written goals.
I keep making the same mistakes.
I feel scattered and overwhelmed with too much going on in my life.

Experience is a hard teacher because she gives the test first, the lesson after.
Vernon S. Law

WHAT IF . . . ?

- I frequently checked my goals to see how I was doing
- I continually learned from my experiences and applied the learning to my life plan
- I had a simple mechanism to monitor my purposefulness

THEN . . .

I would stay on track to achieve my goals. I would feel energetic. I would focus. I would experience life as a win-win game: If I get the result I want, I win; if I do not get the result I want, I learn.

SIMPLY

This chapter focuses on how to develop the habit of using a system, The Results Game, to identify the internal and external results you want in the next few weeks. As a learning game, not a goal-achievement game, you lay the track and subsequently monitor the degree to which you follow it. The purpose of The Results Game is to influence you to take charge of your choices to get the results you want. We call it a *game* because it is a metaphor for life, and life constitutes learning.

Life is what happens
when you are busy making other plans.
John Lennon

There is no failure...only feedback.
Author Unknown

Language is the house of being.
Martin Heidegger, philosopher

LIVE IT

Playing The Results Game rewards you with focus, motivation to move toward your goals, and learning. Both doing and being signify vital aspects of the Game. To play, you record the results you want, live life, then extract the learning—Guidelines for Winning, the discrepancies between what you wanted and what you got. We introduce Next-Action-Step thinking. By playing The Results Game, you banish the type of procrastination that attacks well-being.

UP

The Results Game promotes a macro-perspective because it includes all areas of your life, from career to money to health to spiritual development. Your Guidelines for Winning heighten awareness to bring you to new levels of advancement and UPliftment.

BRIEF SOLUTIONS

1. The Results Game
The game of life comprises order and chaos. With perspective, chaos becomes order. The Results Game offers focused perspective by giving you a structure to order your chaos.
The Cheshire Cat in Alice in Wonderland mysteriously warns Alice, "If you don't know where you are going, **any road** will take you there." Any road is not good enough. Any road can lead to dead ends, detours, continuous rotaries, loops, roundabouts, soft shoulders, or one-way streets. We can learn to choose the road that points in a purposeful direction.

PURPOSES OF THE RESULTS GAME
- Focus and prioritize key results for a three-week period
- Track the thinking process to generate Guidelines for Winning
- Provide a mechanism for monitoring success
- Remind you that life includes both doing and being
- Affirm well-being and acknowledge doing
- Give extra motivation when needed
- Check regularly into all areas of life
- Increase the probability of winning the next game

Results may be *doing results*, such as cleaning the bedroom, or *being results*, such as feeling light as I clean the bedroom. Doing

SUPPLIES NEEDED TO CREATE A RESULTS GAME

- 12 Index cards, 1 for each life area
- Next Action Step list of incomplete items
- Annual committed goals
- Calendar
- Guidelines for Winning

results have clear external measurements. Being results often require a standard of measurement to ascertain if you achieve what you want. To measure a being result, determine how you feel now (current state) and how you want to feel (desired state).

For example, assume you want this result: "Feel relaxed at work." Reflect on how relaxed you feel nowadays, on a scale of 1-10. Let us say you answer "5." Now imagine three weeks in the future at work; how relaxed would you want to feel on a scale of 1-10? You answer "7." This is how this result would appear on a Results Game: I feel relaxed at work (5⇨7).

To create results, use *the product or process approach*. Imagine that you want to read a book you started a long time ago. You could write it either as a process result, "Spend two hours reading," or as a product result, "Read four chapters." Which aligns with your desire? Sometimes we create failure by saying we want to read four chapters when we really want to read for two hours.

People who feel fulfilled and effective have **both** being and doing results. Successful people average about fifteen to nineteen items for a two-to-three-week period. Weekly Results Games do not work because they appear too similar to To Do Lists, which do not allow for the unfoldment of well-being. Monthly Results Games do not work either; they become stale. Two to three weeks is ideal.

We intentionally chose the word *result* instead of goal. You create a goal by experiencing the present and imagining what you desire in the future. Your present may be replete with your limitations and blinders. Therefore, you are creating goals through a lens with limitations and blinders.

GOAL = NOW ⇨⇨⇨ FUTURE

Alternatively, we can choose the perspective of projecting ourselves into our imaginary future and *looking back* at the present. (See "Design Your Own Destiny," Chapter 2) The future need not contain any limitations because it does not yet exist, so, we can create it any way we choose.

RESULT = FUTURE ⇦⇦⇦ NOW

The physical body cannot distinguish fantasy from reality; therefore, you will find it *as easy* to imagine being in the future and looking backward as being in the present looking forward. Use both ways and notice the difference.

Instructions for Creating The Results Game

First, take twelve Life Area Cards and arrange them in order of importance according to the results you want for a two-to-three-week period. **It is very important that this step precede the calen-**

LIFE AREAS

HEALTH
APPEARANCE
FAMILY
FRIENDS
RELATIONSHIP
FUN
HOME
MONEY
CAREER
SERVICE
PERSONAL DEVELOPMENT
SPIRITUAL DEVELOPMENT

SAMPLE RESULTS GAME

For *Debbie Lovejoy*
From *10/8 to 10/29*

Area	#	Items
Health	1	Exercise 3x/week
	2	Take vitamins
Career	3	Finish monthly report on time
	4	Be patient (6⇨8) with boss
Fun	5	Do something zany
	6	Have fun at Pam's party
Home	7	Organize desk files (2 hours)
Personal	8	Say affirmation for confidence
Spiritual	9	Get back into meditation

dar check-in to prevent our calendar (representing current commitments) from driving the process. We easily fill our calendars with "busy"ness that may not be on purpose. Now select the end date for this Results Game.

Second, begin with the top card, and check three databases:
- Past (prioritized Next Action Steps for projects in process)
- Present (calendar commitments)
- Future (Annual Goals)

Write in draft form any key Result (doing or being) that describes what you want to achieve or experience in the period chosen for your Game. Consider every life area, although not every area must have results. One area may have many key results, another, few. Remember The Results Game differs from a To Do List. It contains the **most** important results, those that describe the life we truly want. A typical To Do List identifies only doing, not being. Check that the results are real commitments rather than fanciful wishes. Laying down the track is an important first step.

Third, after drafting results, read your Guidelines for Winning to verify the consistency of your language. You will have your first set of Guidelines only after concluding the time period of your Results Game. Make adjustments. Our Guidelines represent how we think when we win. When we modify our thoughts to harmonize with our Guidelines, we increase the probability of getting what we want.

Fourth, finalize your Results Game, and put it in a place where it is easily visible. We need to keep important things in front of us, so when something urgent pops UP, we can remember we retain the option of choosing the important.

Fifth, live your life to see what it brings.

How To Analyze The Results Game

Schedule twenty minutes on the last day of The Results Game period to compare what you wrote down with what actually happened. Use this time to recognize what you have accomplished and to generate your Guidelines. Review your thought patterns, behaviors, feelings, and habits for each result you did not achieve according to your criteria. Ask why you did not achieve the result. Questions empower you to continue learning, growing, and wondering. These questions may guide you:
- What gets in my way of getting that result?
- What part of not getting my result bothers me?
- What beliefs and attitudes keep me from succeeding?
- What behaviors trip me?

A well-defined life question becomes
a self-correcting life map.
Nelson Zink

Life is full of surprises,
but we don't have to be dumbfounded.
Author Unknown

The only way to pass any test is to take the test.
Author Unknown

- What can I do differently?
- What choice became more important than what I had said I wanted?
- How would I need to feel to get the result?
- How would I coach myself next time given the same or a similar set of circumstances?
- Is my result too general? Too specific?
- Are all or most of my results doing results?
- How would I know if I had achieved this result?
- How could I increase the probability of getting the result?
- What operating principle enables me to get the result?
- What positive things do I notice about how I get results?

Either you achieve a result or you do not. **You receive no partial credit**. You win by getting the result you want, or you win by recognizing an opportunity to learn, *i.e.*, generate Guidelines for Winning for the next time. This is a win-win game.

WRITING GUIDELINES

Write Guidelines like affirmations—Positive, Present tense, and Personalized. Impersonal Guidelines pertain to everyone, such as car bumper stickers, for example: *Speak your truth courageously.* Personalize a Guideline by putting *I, me, myself,* or *my* as part of the statement. The rewritten result reads, *"I speak my truth courageously."*

Own your Guidelines, your gems, the learning treasures you dig UP. You can change your thought processes and behavior by laying the track, learning, and making course adjustments. Use your Guidelines to have fun, win, and experience your winning.

Some of your Guidelines may repeat. If this happens, explore deeper. You may fine-tune the Guideline and gain subtle insights or a new angle. If the same Guideline persists, weave the Guideline into your Results Game and decide what level (1 to 10) you choose to LIVE IT. This feedback loop multiplies the probability of success. Over the course of the next few Results Games, increase the level until you live the way you want.

We have a natural tendency to carry over results we do not achieve into the next game. You may do this twice; however, seriously consider whether to carry over the same result a third time. Not achieving a result usually indicates learning must take place to shift the paradigm from losing to winning. **Life circumstances repeat until we learn from them.** We already know from Chapter 1 that glitch messages continue until we pay attention. View the Results Game as a microcosm of your entire life. Use it to learn to SIMPLY

RESULTS GAME

SCORING STEPS

1. Number each item on your Results Game (*e.g.*, 1, 2, 3, etc.).

2. Check off each item achieved.

To calculate the Overall Percentage Achieved:
    (Total # achieved ÷ total # on game) x 100 = Overall %

To calculate the Priority Percentage Achieved:
    a. Assign importance (priority) points to each item (achieved and not achieved). If you have a total of 8 items; item 1 should be assigned 8 points; item 2 should be assigned 7 points; item 3, 6 points, etc.

    b. Add up the points for those achieved. This is B.

    c. (Total # of items) x (total # of items + 1) ÷ 2 = A.

    d. (B ÷ A) x 100 = Priority %

LIVE IT UP.

You can also extract a Guideline for Winning when you succeed in obtaining a Result. New circumstances and constant changes sometimes cloud memories of successes, so it is equally important to capture the principles that bring success.

Be creative and resourceful with your Guidelines. Record them on your One-der tape (See next page), design a colorful three-dimensional collage, sing your Guidelines to your favorite melody, share them with a close friend, write them for the company newsletter, incorporate them in your dreams....

How to Analyze Results Game Patterns

After eight games (approximately five months), you will have enough data to analyze patterns. Spread out your Results Games chronologically and answer these questions:

- Did the same area top your list each time?
- Review the top three life areas. Do the same ones repeat?
- How often did you achieve the top result? Always? Most of the time? Rarely?
- What is the chance of getting results in your top areas?
- Do you notice a pattern in consistently missing life areas?

By analyzing your Results Game patterns, you can form useful strategies for future games. For example, if your analysis reveals consistent success in the top three items, place results that require extra motivation there, where you will be likely to get them. Eventually, you will develop criteria for designing your games.

Keep your Results Games! Employ The Results Games for self-acknowledgment. They represent your autobiography, your journal of success. When you feel down or unproductive, pull out your Results Games to substantiate your successes. Your Games map your learning path.

How To Score The Results Game

We assign two scores to the Game—the **overall percentage** and the **priority percentage.** Calculate the overall percentage by taking the number of results you accomplish and dividing it by the total number on the Game. However, this score does not allow for your rank-ordered life areas. So, we also recommend calculating a priority percentage. The **priority percentage** allots more credit to the ones at the top of The Results Game (that we rank as more important) than the ones at the bottom. To obtain percentages, see page 72.

SAMPLE GUIDELINES FOR WINNING

1. I feel better when I keep my word.

2. When I relax, I accomplish my results.

3. My results are specific yet allow for options.

4. Putting something on my list is only the first step, then I need to act.

5. In order for me to actualize results, I need adequate preparation time.

6. When I allow time, I can appreciate the adventure.

7. In order for me to know where I am going, I need to know what is in my way.

8. I ask myself what experience I want before I commit to action.

9. I am motivated when I am emotionally connected to something.

10. I remember to take a moment to ask myself, "What do I really want?"

Guidelines contributed by Linda Klevans
and Jennifer Merritt

TIP: Imagine a traditional To Do list. At first glance, the unfinished items leap out. We usually cross off accomplished items. So, every time we look at our To Do list, we see what we still need to do. By crossing off an item, our "child-mind" feels invalidated. The "child within" manages our well-being. It is paramount to affirm, highlight, acknowledge, and validate our achievements. We need to find a filter that beckons us to focus on our successes first, instead of failures and incompletes. If we highlight a result after we get it, we see the highlighting over and over and continually acknowledge ourselves. Each time we look at our Game, we first notice the highlighted items. Only after, do we notice the items not highlighted. We can be patient about those we did not accomplish because we see them through the visor of success.

Highlighting works! It will remind you of your successes and increase your sense of well-being. We recommend using several colors (no color coding necessary) to symbolize the colors of the rainbow as you harvest pots of gold (your success and well-being).

2. Your One-der Tape

To create a personal subliminal tape, use an external microphone to record your own voice while dubbing Classical Baroque music, largo beat, from one tape cassette to another. Or you might tape record the Guidelines in your own voice with music coming from a second source such as a record, a CD, or another tape. The volume of the music needs to be slightly louder than the words.

Make the content rich by adding life purpose, inspiring visions, and affirmations to your tape. Guidelines for Winning make wonderful gifts to your more-than-conscious mind. Check that your tape only includes messages written in positive, present tense, personalized statements.

Your own tape has a great chance of working because tapes you prepare contain what you feel ready to receive. Imagine the power of listening to your voice speaking current and relevant information. When you invite this into your more-than-conscious mind, the effect multiplies. Clients who listen to their self-made One-der tapes report a high degree of success.

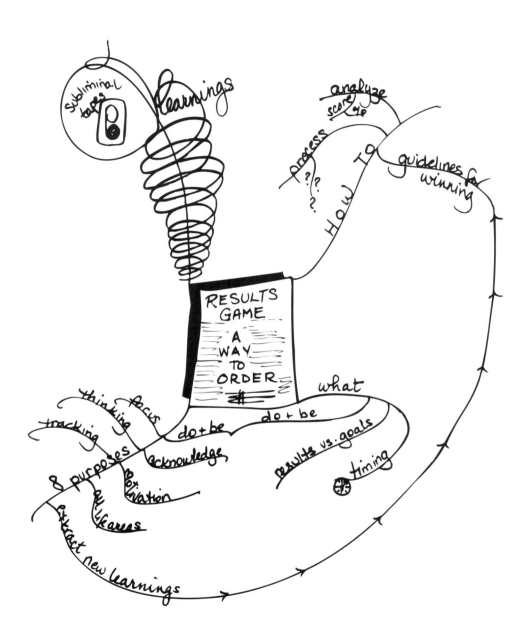

subliminal tapes

learnings

analyze
score
progress
?.?
?.?
HOW TO

guidelines for winning

RESULTS GAME
A WAY TO ORDER #

what

thinking
focus
tracking
do + be
do + be
acknowledge
8 purposes
motivation
all areas
results vs. goals
timing
extract new learnings

LIST OF BRIEF SOLUTIONS for Chapter 4

1. The Results Game and Guidelines for Winning
2. Your One-der Tape

ACTION

How do I intend to apply these solutions to my life to get the results I want?

What Next Action Step do I plan to take?

Although The Results Game includes well-being items, there is more to learn about influencing and monitoring your well-being. The next chapter introduces another game, **The Well-Being Game**, that encourages you to learn about the facets of your being.

SIMPLY LIVE IT UP

CHAPTER 5

THE WELL-BEING GAME

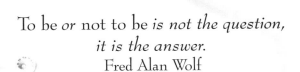

To be *or* not to be *is not the question,*
it is the answer.
Fred Alan Wolf

The best things in life are—just things.
Hallmark mug

Focus on creating responsive relationships among all the parts of you. Honoring the diversity within you is the beginning of the possibility of synergy. Prioritize periods of UNprogrammed time (rest, re-creation, reflection). They allow you to develop wisdom, balance, and communication with your inner Self, and to sustain your ability to experience wholeness in an ever-changing world.
Charles Parry
Peak Performance Coach

CHAPTER 5

THE WELL-BEING GAME

PROBLEM

I am more comfortable doing than being.
I don't know much about my being Self.
I feel victim to my being. I don't know how to influence myself.
I never feel as if I'm doing enough.

The proportion of being to doing determines your life character.
Nelson Zink

WHAT IF . . . ?

- I influenced my well-being
- I paid attention to how I felt and experienced life
- My well-being became more important than my doing

THEN . . .

I would be the driver instead of feeling driven. I would be in touch with my feelings and could use them to detect and choose purposeful opportunities. I would love the being part of living.

SIMPLY

The Well-Being Game enables you to identify aspects of your being, how to access your well-being through your intuition, and how to track and influence well-being with your reticular system.

LIVE IT

The Well-Being Game provides valuable information about the facets of internal experience so you can experience and influence your being. It reveals whether you need to get results to feel successful or whether you use success as a motivator to get results. It also helps you access and trust your intuition.

I'm convinced success in general comes from two major sources, consistency and goals. Consistency means treating every challenge the same, whether it's a practice run or a run for the Olympic Gold Medal. Getting good at things by practice - practice - practice is what improves one's performance. Every personal best I ever achieved became it's own motivation to do better, which led me to greater effort. Once I tasted it, I wanted it more, so I focused my efforts. I began setting goals for myself. Little goals. First it was seconds, then tenths of a second, then hundredths of a second. Twice I won Gold Medals by two hundredths of a second—proof that we must recognize and honor even our smallest triumphs. The truest and most important motivation to keep trying comes from inside. I can control my attitude. That's the most important element I can bring to the starting line. I can give it my all.

Bonnie Blair
Winner of 5 Olympic Gold Medals for Speed Skating

UP

Awareness of being can expand your sense of Self so that you can conceive of "being results," not just "doing results" in your game of life. When you are in doing mode, you achieve in order to feel finished or accomplished. From one perspective, the ultimate accomplishment of life means death; therefore, there must be more to life than accomplishing. Focusing on being opens the gateway from dying to living.

BRIEF SOLUTION: The Well-Being Game

The Well-Being Game can make you aware of the important facets of your well-being. Most people feel adept at writing doing statements and tracking goals, yet they may not know how to monitor being.

PURPOSES OF THE WELL-BEING GAME
- Recognize the qualities that describe well-being
- Distinguish those qualities out of balance and those with a great degree of influence
- Note the constant qualities, those you can count on no matter what the external circumstances. (We call these qualities "friends")
- Pinpoint qualities with large fluctuations, those that suggest reaction to circumstances ("roller coasters")
- Highlight the correlation between your well-being and your ability to produce results
- Experience awareness of the being part of life
- Remember your well-being, even when all goes well
- Record qualities that increase as you place your reticular system on them ("staircase")

SUPPLIES NEEDED
A chart with 12 to 14 graphs, each having ten divisions on the left side representing intensity and at least eight divisions at the bottom representing intervals of two to three weeks each, and highlighters.

INSTRUCTIONS FOR CREATING THE WELL-BEING GAME
Recall yourself in a state of well-being. Name 12 to 14 qualities that describe you. Write one at the top of each graph. Reflect on the interval of your last Results Game. Ask yourself, "How much did I feel this quality during this time on a scale of 1 to 10?" High-

*The essential philosophical quest in the world
is for integration, which is to say,
the need to bring together rational philosophy,
spiritual belief, scientific knowledge,
personal experience, and direct observation
into an organic whole.*
Norman Cousins
*The Celebration of Life:
A Dialogue on Immortality and Infinity*

*There is nothing either good or bad,
but thinking makes it so.*
William Shakespeare

SIMPLY LIVE IT UP

How do you know what number to put down? The numbers come from your intuition and inner knowing. Respect the accuracy of the data, even if you do not believe you have a highly developed intuition. The source of the ratings may be initially puzzling. Just let the numbers emerge.

TIP: If you find yourself attached to specific events, imagine floating five feet above a horizontal line with numbers *1* to *10* on it. Begin at *1* and float along the line until you hesitate. That number describes the level of well-being for the quality under consideration.

Our intuition serves as a practical tool. Become familiar with your intuitive ability by accessing and trusting it in this game.

How to Analyze The Well-Being Game

The numbers you collect for your well-being help you to identify your current state. Consider having a friend highlight your qualities for you, thereby minimizing your natural tendency to depend upon your recent and past ratings as you consider the present.

Look at the range of numbers. Do you use the full range? A small range? Note whether you chose any *10's*. If not, have you not experienced a *10*, or do you not allow yourself to have one? At the time you created the Game, you could not imagine more than a *10*. As your well-being increases, you may break the barrier to realize that more than *10* seems possible. Your standards change. Welcome to the world of *11's!*

Shoe sizes explain breaking the barrier. Children's shoe sizes in the U.S.A. number UP to *13*, where adult sizes begin. Same numbering system, yet the numbers mean something different. A child size *7* is much smaller than an adult size *7*. The numbers themselves have no inherent value because men's shoes and women's shoes both have size *7*, which differ as well. Numbers reflect relative sizes.

> Nick obtained a fairly low percentage of results, yet his well-being scored high. He pondered the source of his well-being: he discovered he enjoyed the process of getting the results and learning, more than obtaining the goal. Now Nick can intentionally increase his well-being by focusing on process; whereas before, he only knew how to focus on outcome.

Both doing and being influence our sense of Self. Acknowledge yourself for doing and affirm yourself for being. Compare the range of results against the range of well-being. Some people get

Just do it beautifully!
Charlotte Ward

Dissolving the mind is a matter of not-doing.
Brian Walker
Hua Hu Ching: The Unknown Teachings of Lao Tzu

Prior preparation prevents poor performance.
Author Unknown

results but have low well-being. Others experience the reverse. Still others demonstrate no relationship between the two. You need not judge the data, SIMPLY use the information to design your destiny.

Over time, with seven or more pieces of data, you will begin to discern patterns, such as friend, roller coaster, and staircase.

FRIEND

Like friends, some qualities support you. Stable well-being qualities remain constant despite external circumstances or internal thoughts. You can count on these parts of yourself. It feels good to know you have friends.

ROLLER COASTER

The roller-coaster pattern fluctuates without any obvious increasing or decreasing trends. This volatile part surges with the course of internal or external events. Sometimes a roller coaster theme suggests uncertainty about the word you selected. Information about your mutable qualities plays into your life design.

STAIRCASE

The third pattern shows UP like a staircase with an occasional deviation. You may discard one extreme piece of data in considering the whole picture. To detect the staircase, look at the first half of the chart, then the second half, and compare the average of the two halves. If the average of the second looks greater than the first, you have an ascending staircase trend.

Rarely will you find a decreasing pattern because you know that when you put your awareness on something, you experience it.

The reticular system (See Chapter 1) functions like a television channel selector; a channel of focus. Imagine watching Channel 4. You know that Channel 5 exists out there—somewhere, yet until you change channels, you cannot see it or hear it. Assuming abundance of everything on this planet, if you tune to a particular channel, you put your awareness on it and experience it. I often put my reticular system on four leaf clovers and find them in the most unimaginable places.

Your thoughts create reality. If you allow incompletes to consume your energy, (See Chapter 7), you may find it difficult to effectively use your reticular system. For example, imagine that you need a new car. You decide to purchase a Honda. Suddenly, you notice all the Hondas on the road, right? They are not coming out of hiding. They have been there all along, yet your reticular system had not been tuned to the Honda channel.

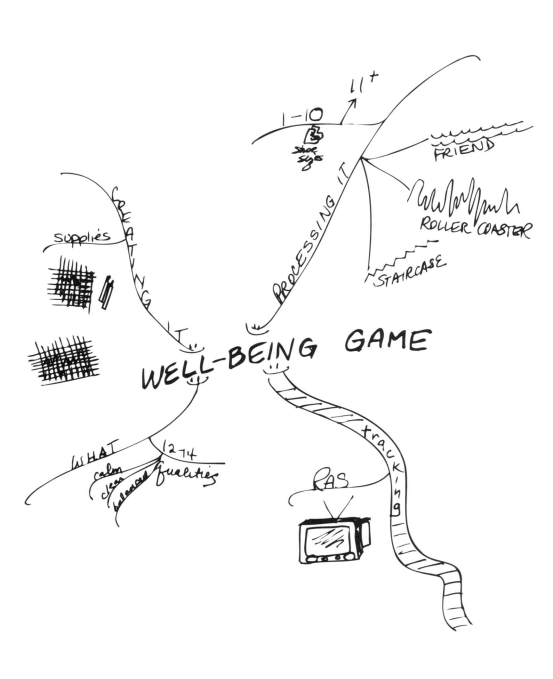

WELL-BEING GAME

1-10 → 11+
STOCK
SYS

PROCESSING IT

FRIEND

ROLLER COASTER

STAIRCASE

CREATING IT

supplies

WHAT
12-14
calm
clear
balanced
qualities

tracking

RAS

You experience power when you combine intention with your reticular system. Program it for any of the senses: auditory, visual, olfactory, touch, or taste. Direct your being on *confidence* for two weeks, and notice what happens!

How to Apply The Well-Being Game

- Create *being* results on your next Results Game.
- Use your well-being qualities in business every chance you get, for example, in your brochures, cover letters, resumes, office memos, and introductions to speeches and workshops. Use them in your personal life on party invitations, thank-you notes....

> For Todd's retirement party Mary incorporated his purpose—*Courageously explore options to bring balance and peace.* On the invitations, she wrote, "Come join Todd for his courageous transition. Bring your peaceful self and potluck options!"

- Sprinkle your qualities into your everyday language. These words are YOU. You increase your well-being the more you use them.

You can influence your well-being. **Be**-gin now!

BRIEF SOLUTION for Chapter 5: The Well-Being Game

ACTION

How do I intend to apply this solution to my life to get the results I want?

What Next Action Step do I plan to take?

Both The Results Game and The Well-Being Game highlight personal growth and development and your experience of winning. Part of winning continuously comes from perceiving time as a friend instead of a foe. The next chapter, **It's About Time**, explores the relationship of time to your Well-Being, namely healing yourself from dis-ease and living your ideal week.

SIMPLY LIVE IT UP

CHAPTER 6
IT'S ABOUT TIME

Even the heart rests.
Charlotte Ward

A TEMPO
A Work in Progress

*I know better atemporal time sky time dream time cloud time
in the cup of your hands in the night night night of no time
hope for a winter storm hope for snow time jazz time bliz-
zards of minutes hours seconds piled high on the sills until
everything outside stands still blow kisses in the whispered
white time in the still close space of a cocoon*

Tempo: One and two and keep the beat and
Who how when where oh what then?
Step in time through Purgatory
Live forever without sin
Hallelujah Hallelujah!
Ah-men Ah-men!

I am learning to use time productively.

*I know better atemporal time sargasso on the foam of past
present future afloat in mesmerizing rhythm with the moon
do I care what time it is that the wild swans come and go I
know better atemporal time where no one is late and the circle
is complete in the image heave a sigh of relief where lost is
found and being is being I know better atemporal time than
real time whatever that is*

Tempo: One and two and keep the beat and
Who how when where oh what then?
Step in time through Purgatory
Live forever without sin
Hallelujah Hallelujah!
Ah-men Ah-men!

Continued on page 94

CHAPTER 6

IT'S ABOUT TIME

PROBLEM

I don't have enough time.
Sometimes I feel as if time stops.
There are times when I feel time is lost.
Why can't I be on time?
I hate standing in line and waiting.

> *Time is just nature's way of making sure*
> *that everything doesn't happen all at once.*
> Ziggy

WHAT IF . . . ?

- Time were irrelevant to the course of my events
- I controlled my time and made it conform to my needs
- I had enough time
- I related to learning and healing as the same thing

THEN . . .

I would have time to live a balanced life and do all those things I value. I would feel free to take time for myself. I would relate differently to dis-ease. Overall, I would make choices according to my internal messages instead of the clock. I would experience living as a natural flow.

SIMPLY

This chapter deals with unwrapping the tangled web of temporal contradictions. You design your Ideal Week by setting down your schedule wishes for future living.

LIVE IT

You can treat time like a friend. By viewing time as internal instead of external, you can deal with it from a place of integrity. By

I am learning to give quality time.

Real time is what everyone is talking about how to raise a brighter child in 20 minutes a day wasting in spite of resolutions stretching like a rubber band around last year's check stubs saving any way possible throwing up sandbags against the inevitable tide inconsequential in the heave of a mountain swell of a sea

At the time the tone will be *a tempo*

Ha there must be a holographic God watching us run our time-line mazes laughing through time laughing that we all got the same number two billion heartbeats laughing to welcome us when we come round again I feel his belly shake the bare ground and the waters tremble

I know better atemporal time fossil time moss time Everest time mother and baby time music time poetry time precious time in tempo with the right brain of the universe.

Charlotte Ward

living in the moment, time vanishes, and you may feel as if you exist independent of it. Once you create your Ideal Week, you can take one step at a time toward living it.

UP

Time heals all wounds, bringing back a state of love. Time insures perspective on events.

BRIEF SOLUTIONS

1. Heal Thyself Now
Healing has absolutely nothing to do with time. Both healing and disease take place in an instant.

> I was sunk rather deeply in a depression today. It started with a wake-up headache. I thought that by taking aspirins and getting outside, I'd eliminate both the headache and the depression. Of course, they both kept me company all the more tenaciously. I'm coming to understand that depression is not different from illness with respect to being a teacher. In order to learn, it was necessary to experience it respectfully and lovingly.
>
> So, I let myself brood. I allowed myself to release that tether and take no action. I simply let the blues and the headache be in all their glory, just as I let the low-pressure weather of the day be. I would not fight them or myself and would be gifted by whatever they taught. I was going to have to be courageous, meeting all the players of the universe on their own terms, allowing space for them to be and do, and finally learning from and loving them all.
>
> Kristin Lake
> P.S. Headache is gone.

For the past twenty years, I have used my own healing process to bring me to that moment when dis-ease is ready to leave my body. People call me an amazing self-healer. I SIMPLY take these steps:

- When I feel the slightest bit of dis-ease, I stop to take quiet time. This step sometimes challenges me. I continue my pace of activity, pretend nothing is wrong, and resist getting sick. "I can't get sick now," I hear my panicky self-talk assert. Now, I allow the "germ" to visit me.

In/HABIT yourself.
Kate Melvin

All life is an experiment.
Oliver Wendall Holmes

Awareness of time implies perspective and judgment.
Charlotte Ward

Go faster by going slower.
Author Unknown

SIMPLY LIVE IT UP

- While it visits, I ask it for a message. It visits me for a reason, and I want to learn why. I patiently listen for a response. I relax. I experience myself flowing in and out of my multidimensional levels of reality. All levels participate in self-healing.
- Although I find appreciating being sick challenging, I thank the germ for being. I have discovered that genuine gratitude quickens the healing process. Make sure you experience deep gratitude, or this process will not work.
- The final step allows the dis-ease to move on. Allow it, not force or demand—allow.

Do I get sick? Of course, I do. However, it may take me two hours to move through a week-long flu, or five minutes for a bad cold or sore throat. Experiment. You can do it too!

2. Exaggeration Day, or SIMPLY, how to get back into regular exercise.
People frequently use the excuse that they do not have time to exercise. We present a Brief Solution guaranteed to get you back into exercise without taking much time. Have an Exaggeration Day.

An Exaggeration Day means exaggerate every motion you make. For example, when you reach the phone to make a call, withdraw your hand, then reach again, withdraw. Do this several times. Try these motions, then create your own.
- When you drop a piece of paper on the floor, bend down and UP several times before you actually pick UP the paper.
- Yawn with a full arm sweep, and repeat.
- Pick UP your briefcase a few times.
- Do deep knee bends while waiting at the copy machine.
- Lift the bag of groceries front and back and UP and down before putting it into the car.

By the end of the day, you will have exercised so that you may not have to go to the gym. You will likely get back into a regular exercise because you have already taken the hardest step—the first step—SIMPLY exaggerating your natural movements.

3. Priority Shifts
We have replaced our inner sense of time with an external mechanism. We listen to the clock instead of our body's natural rhythms. We eat because it is noon, without even checking inside to see if we are hungry.

*The world is moving so fast these days
that the man who says it can't be done
is generally interrupted by someone doing it.*
Harry Emerson Fosdick

I'm lost, but I'm making record time.
A pilot, somewhere over the Pacific

Practice the Pause

*Practice the pause. When in doubt,
p r a c t i c e   t h e   p a u s e .   W h e n
angry, practice the pause. When tired,
practice   the   pause. When
stressed, practice the pause.*

*Breathe   Clear the mind View   from
        a   Different Perspective
                 Smile Laugh Sleep Dream Breathe
Even the heart rests.*

Charlotte Ward,
inspired by Reverend Martin Lowenthal, Ph.D.

During a leisurely visit, my friend Thom and I ruminated on the frantic pace of existence around us. He mischievously led me on a time warp adventure. We planted ourselves in the middle of the Newark train station, where the suburban and city trains, the local and express buses, and the morning commuters zoom by. People were running in all directions, bumping into each other without even noticing it, not smiling—not apologizing for collisions, not speaking at all. Swept up in smoky channels of light beams, commuters vigorously swirled in all directions, like autumn leaves escaping a leaf blowing machine.

When we face a natural disaster, we let go of our schedules and priorities. During a flood, hurricane, or snowstorm, people tend to eat when they feel hungry and sleep when they feel tired. Tune into your natural internal rhythm as the song from *Annie, Get Your Gun* tells us, "doin' a what comes naturally," even when your life is running smoothly.

4. Your Ideal Week
How would you design a week to meet your ideal specifications? Most people live a very different week from their ideal. To live your Ideal Week, be clear about the way you do spend your time, as well as the way you would like to. Take these steps:
- Rank the areas of your life according to your values (See page 52).
- Order your life areas according to how much time you spend on the average in a week. If your career consumes most of your time, place it at the top.
- Look at the two lists. Are any of the areas three or more apart in rank order? This suggests an improper balance and an opportunity to adjust. As you create your Ideal Week, check that the ones you placed higher on the value list receive sufficient time.
- Take a weekly calendar and block off time slots for your #1 ranked value life area. For example: Assume that Health is your #1 value life area. How much time each week do you want to allocate for activities that support your health? When would you like to be doing these activities? Consider which activities juxtapose well for balance.

TIP: If activities, such as phone calls to family, take brief moments several times a week, group the time slots to insure avail-

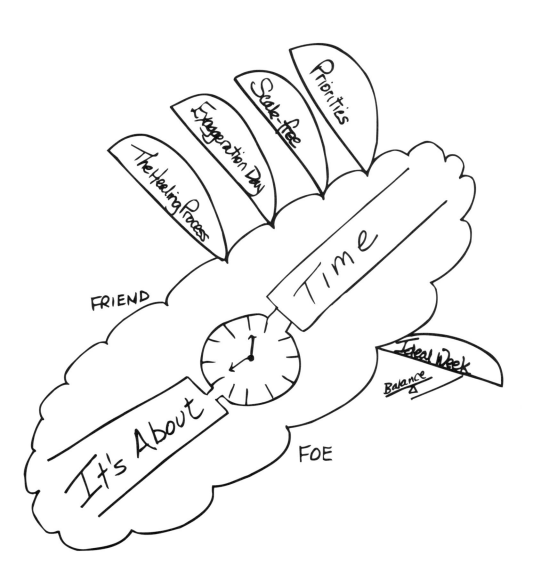

able time. Calls need not occur then, just be sure to allot enough time.

CAUTION: If you find yourself recording current reality rather than allowing the ideal scene to come forth, ask yourself, "What do I **really** want?"

> Julie wanted to exercise three times a week at six o'clock, yet with her new baby, she needed to stay home until daycare opened. The gym did not open until seven. Once she identified what she wanted, she came up with a new possibility. She posted a sign on the community bulletin board. Two other women, eager to begin exercise at that hour, agreed to come to Julie's house. They showed an exercise video in the basement, and Julie used an intercom to listen for her baby. Everybody felt successful.

Just by identifying what you want, you UP your probability of getting it!

LIST OF BRIEF SOLUTIONS for Chapter 6

1. Heal Thyself Now
2. Exaggeration Day
3. Priority Shifts
4. Your Ideal Week

ACTION

How do I intend to apply these solutions to my life to get the results I want?

What Next Action Step do I plan to take?

This chapter looked at ways you can relate to time as an ally. Your Ideal Week may appear impossible because you have a plethora of projects and overwhelming responsibilities. When new things emerge, you may tend to demote your incompletes to the back burner. Chapter 7, **What Do You Do with Broken Umbrellas**, presents a system for you to resurrect and manage your unfinished business so you can live your Ideal Week.

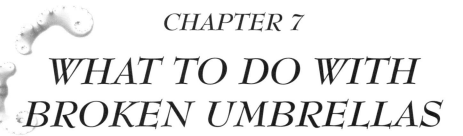

CHAPTER 7
WHAT TO DO WITH BROKEN UMBRELLAS

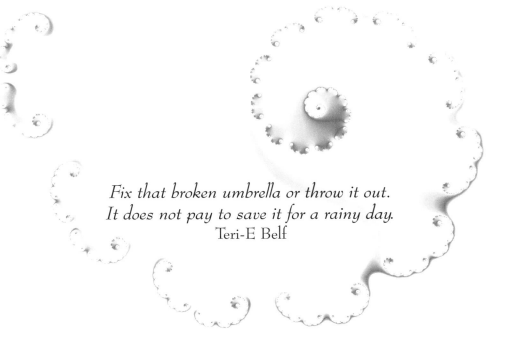

Fix that broken umbrella or throw it out.
It does not pay to save it for a rainy day.
Teri-E Belf

Any umbrellas, any umbrellas to mend today?
He'll mend your parasol,
it may be small, it may be big.
He'll mend them all
with what he calls his thingamajig.
Sung by Bing Crosby

SIMPLY LIVE IT UP

CHAPTER 7

WHAT TO DO WITH BROKEN UMBRELLAS

PROBLEM

I have scraps of paper all over.
My house is a mess. My files and desk are disorganized.
My closets, rooms, _____ are cluttered.
                    Fill in the blank

> *You've let the lawn go too far when it requires harvesting.*
> Doug Larson

WHAT IF . . . ?

- I fixed all the "broken umbrellas" in my life
- I chose to unpack the cartons in the attic and basement
- I cleaned the garage
- I paid my overdue parking tickets and back taxes
- I took time out for myself

THEN . . .

My word would be good because I would do what I have been saying I was going to do. I would finish my "unfinished business." I would bring my "back-burner" items to the front burner. I would feel in charge of my life. I would allow myself to have fun. If I were to die unexpectedly, my affairs would all be in order.

SIMPLY

"Broken umbrellas" signifies those things in your life you have started but never finished. "Someday I will get that umbrella fixed," yet, for efficiency, you buy a new one, without throwing away the broken one because MAYBE SOMEDAY you will run into the umbrella repair person.

You can learn to increase your productivity and effectiveness. This chapter presents a system for creating space in your life—physical and mental. The Brief Solutions put you in charge of your

Prime orderliness is life's first law.
David Seabury

Sometimes simple not so easy.
Chinese saying

projects, even those that have been around for a long time, called "Moldy Oldies." In this chapter you learn to list your current projects in one place and eliminate many scraps of paper. The solutions introduce strategies for mentally spring cleaning, for identifying projects in terms of prioritized Next Action Steps, for handling incompletes and unfinished business, and, for acknowledging yourself every step along the way. We need a solution to cope with the Information Age, with cyclones of paper and technological data in every corner. **This solution works.**

LIVE IT

Simplifying life means clearly choosing what you want to spend your time on, and when.

> After my accident, the insurance company ruled my car was totaled. I wanted to save it, so I easily gathered and faxed eight years of repair and maintenance receipts to make a case for its value. Ten minutes later the insurance representative agreed to save the car. Because I am organized, I have choices in life, and, I 'm likely to get what I want.

When you organize, you get what you want!

UP

Open your broken umbrella in the rain and look UP. Not functional, is it? You focus your attention on avoiding raindrops in your eyes instead of enjoying the broader view under dry shelter. Life's broken umbrellas create limited perspectives by impinging on our mental and physical space, thereby obstructing our awareness of the whole. Making space facilitates you to SIMPLY LIVE IT UP.

BRIEF SOLUTIONS

1. The Productivity Cycle
How can you get out of the habit of procrastinating and into the habit of only starting what you will finish? To answer that question, you need to complete the productivity cycle.

Productivity is a ***completed*** cycle of action. Five steps comprise the cycle, each one required, and each required in sequence.

Muddy water when still becomes clear.
Ira Progoss
The Well and the Cathedral

Eliminate mental muddiness...keep your mind
crystal clear.
Hua Hu Ching The Unknown Teachings of Lao Tzu
Brian Walker

Stillness in a swirling world
calls for a certain courage and willingness
to take risks and reach out beyond the rational.
Bill Issacs

Self-expression must pass into communication
for its fulfillment.
Pearl S. Buck

A. STILLNESS

Stillness begins the cycle of doing and being. Stillness fosters internal connection with oneself and brings centered connections with others. An object at rest contains more magnetic force than one constantly moving. To attract anything, we must connect to our still magnetic essence.

B. CONNECTION

We move into the cycle by connecting with the external world. If we do nothing with our ideas and tell no one, nothing happens, and we clearly do not produce. So, to be productive, we must connect with other people. After making the connection, we have to take focused action.

C. ACTION

The third step in the cycle includes bottom-line actions that typically define productivity. Which actions lead to productivity? Try this exercise: Identify the most important thing you did in a recent job. Then ask, "How did I do that?" or "Specifically, what did I do?" Continue with this line of questioning until you can go no further.

You probably end with writing (typing and other written forms of communication) or talking (speaking, verbal and nonverbal communicating). We share ideas by writing and talking, the two actions that effect productivity. Talking and writing comprise the third step in the productivity cycle.

This holds true for every job, from artist to CEO of a large corporation. A sculptor, who, at first glance, seems productive without writing or speaking, nevertheless progresses through the cycle. After ideas emerge, the medium (clay, marble, bronze) must be found or purchased, usually involving asking for supplies (talking) or paying by check or credit card (writing in disguise). We can even view the art of sculpting as three-dimensional writing.

A business organization, from CEO to receptionist, conforms to this model as well. The CEO strategically plans for the future of the company, yet, if no writing or talking occurred, the business would go bankrupt. The CEO needs to inform the executive team of new directions and visions (through talking and writing). The receptionist screens visitors and types memos into the computer. Both positions in the organization rely on talking and writing to impact bottom line productivity. Analyze your job, too!

D. COMPLETION

Completion means acting to the point you feel finished.

*What would you attempt to do if you knew
you could not fail?*
Robert Schuller

*If there are no incompletes in your life,
you might as well lock up the coffin
and say good-bye.*
David Allen

Education is an attitude, not just an acquisition.
Thomas Alva Edison

*The mind is not a vessel to be filled
but a fire to be ignited.*
Plutarch

When you feel finished, you have. Those who stay stuck in the cycle of action and do not complete, do not produce. They become candidates for high blood pressure, heart problems, ulcers, anxiety, and other dis-eases. From the fourth step, completion, we progress to the final step, often overlooked, yet equally important—review and acknowledgment.

E. Review and Acknowledgment

Although many people who complete something feel finished and proceed immediately to the next idea or the next project, they also need to review. The review can be a quick one—"I had this idea, this is what I did, and I finished"—or an extensive evaluation. Similarly, you can acknowledge yourself by SIMPLY taking a deep breath while thinking, "Good for me, I'm done, I did the best I could." Or you can reward yourself with a trip around the world. Whatever the magnitude of reward, review and acknowledge because your creations improve when you affirm your well-being.

2. Mental Spring Cleaning

Every incomplete demands attention and consumes energy. Because we have a finite amount, why deplete yours on incompletes and deny yourself using it in creative ways?

Organizing your mind begins the process of organizing your life. Mental spring cleaning produces the same delightful payoffs as physically cleaning your house. In our Productivity Coaching Program we ask people to begin by generating a Master List of Incompletes. Most people can expect between four and six pages.

Why torture yourself by writing down four to six pages of what you have not yet finished? Every incomplete commands attention from the brain and drains energy that could be available for something else. Your brain cannot function at full capacity if you have a full storage bin of incompletes. Free UP brain space for positive and creative thoughts, instead of tying down these storage bins with unnecessary incompletes, should's, and someday-maybe's. Our brain is not meant to store incompletes. Our brains are meant to provide us with vision, creative imagination, and the ability to be present in scanning environmental and internal stimuli for making choices.

Living requires space—emotional space and physical space. We use some of our allotted space in the process of living as we commit time and energy to our calendar obligations. Moving items are in process. Stuck items are not in process. We call the latter *incompletes*. Inaction consumes our psychic energy. Overdue incompletes, Moldy Oldies, have been around for a long time. They zap the most energy,

Life is full and overflowing with the new,
but it is necessary to empty out the old
in order to make room for the new to enter.
Eileen Caddy

The horizon leans forward offering you space
to place new steps of change.
Maya Angelou
"On the Pulse of the Morning"

Open the doors so the wind can blow away the must.
My house is finally clean, sparkling with fresh air.
It is empty...but filled with sunshine.
Ruth E. Rhodes
"Emptiness"

I call it Now Therapy©. *I say to myself,*
NOW, NOW, NOW.
It keeps me from procrastinating.
Allison Binder Marshak

robbing self-esteem, depleting our energy, and eroding our well-being. With too many Moldy Oldies, we cannot fully participate in the richness of life we deserve.

We need space for new things to come in. If I came to your door and told you that you have just won a huge new refrigerator/freezer and I am here to install it now, you would probably say, "Terrific, give me a few minutes to move the old one." My response, "Sorry, if you do not have the space now, I will go to somebody else who has space for it."

Has this ever happened to you? Have you missed an opportunity because you "had no space"?

> The first time I met Phil, I was eligible for a romantic relationship, whereas, he was involved with someone else. Four years later we met again. He was available, not I. Then, we met a third time. Both eligible and available, we happily married.

Having items in process is fine—the continual process of generating incompletions and completing them defines living. Can you stretch your imagination to conceive of an entire year in which you had nothing going on or in process? It sounds more like death than life. However, if something remains incomplete for too long, it is no longer in process but stuck. We have no objective measurement for the difference between being in process and being stuck. Being stuck is a feeling—an inner awareness of the difficulty to proceed. When stuck, we no longer have that energy available to use. Our creative mind requires energy to play. We also rely upon our energy to declare intentions and design our destiny. If you allow incompletes to consume your energy, you may find it difficult to effectively use your reticular system (See Chapter 1).

Next, we need to explore *SHOULD'S*, and procrastination.

SHOULD INCOMPLETES
Should's carry negative emotional energy. They bring heavy, burdensome feelings. Every area of life can have *should's*. Familiar?

-I should return the book I borrowed.
-I should get back to exercising.
-I should get more sleep.
-I should stop smoking, eating sweets, drinking....
-I should put the photos into the album.

PROCRASTINATION: A FRIEND

INCOMPLETION TRIGGER LIST

1. One item per line. Do not number them
2. Date the list
3. Items can be huge or very specific, anything

WORK, PROFESSIONAL

Desk (on it, in it)
Professional organizations
Projects started
Projects to start
Work environment, ambiance
Manual files and records
Computer files and records
Storage
Systems: repair, enhance
Equipment
Supplies
Financial matters
Licenses
Legal matters
People to call
People to write
Feedback to deliver
Feedback to get
Follow-up, pending
Reports/proposals
  Budget
  MIS
  Personnel
Planning
Meetings: preparation
Info you need
Info someone else needs
Work you're waiting for
Materials waiting for
Telephone

PERSONAL

Items borrowed from, lent to
Health, vitamins, exercise
Storage, attic, garage, basement
Pets, vets
Travel plans, tickets, luggage
Health appointments
Books to read, library books due
Magazines to order, cancel
Gifts, presents, thank you notes
Car: tune-ups, checkups, repairs
Sports equipment, hobbies
Appliances: TV, VCR, toaster
Civic involvements
Equipment, tools
Clubs, associations, church
Outdoors, yard
Projects started, projects to start
Desk (on it, in it), computer
Professional organizations
Birthdays, anniversaries
Financial matters, legal affairs
Bank accounts: savings, checking
Debts, loans, investments, taxes
Insurance: car, health, life
On Order (4-6 weeks delivery)
People to call, write
Closets, drawers, clothes (sort)
Tailors, umbrellas, jewelry
Shoes: polish, heels, dye
Parking tickets
Photo album, picture frames
Living spaces, furniture, decor
Carpenter, plumber, electrical
Items to purchase, give away

You do not always make a bad choice by procrastinating. Sometimes it serves a positive purpose. People who delay overt action may be subliminally clarifying. During their clarification downtime, a chunk of their project may germinate. Thinking, even subliminal processing, is actually a form of action. Honor your multidimensional process!

> Paul found himself waiting until the last moment to write—then suddenly overflowing with words—finally productive, even if just hours before his project deadline. By procrastinating, Paul preserves in-the-moment freshness in his speeches.

If your well-being remains intact, you do not have a problem. Celebrate and honor your operating procedure. It works for you. You finished the job on time. So what if you came through in the last moment. You came through!

If you feel exhausted and miserable and judge yourself for having done it in this way, you do have a problem. Procrastination is not inherently evil unless it negatively impacts your well-being.

PROCRASTINATION: A FOE

> Norm had to negotiate two buses and a trolley to get to our meetings. The police had booted and towed his car two years earlier. Because he did not pay the fine, he owed interest as well. He abandoned his car and bought a motorcycle. After receiving a ticket on his motorcycle, he feared using it, thinking that the police would also impound it. His whole life centered around transportation frustrations and fear of going to jail.

Use your well-being to judge whether you reside on the positive side or the negative side of procrastination.

Ready to springboard into action with your List of Incompletes?
- Date the list so you know when you generated these items.
- Remember your purpose in creating the list is to empty your brain of every item incomplete or in-process.
- As you look at each trigger, write down anything that comes to mind, for example, a big item—*Plan my retirement*; a general item—*Organize my office*; or a specific item—*Call Sabrina*. When you read a specific trigger—*Pets*, and you

The perfect point of procrastination:
when you wait long enough without doing anything,
the job evaporates.
Allen van Emmerik

Sandwich every bit of criticism
between two layers of praise.
Mary Kay Ash

If you correct your mind,
the rest of your life will fall into place.
Brian Walker
Hua Hu Ching: The Unknown Teachings of Lao Tzu

Remember to turn the page.
Grace Murphy

remember you promised to copy a tape for your brother, write down *Tape for brother*. Remember the purpose of this exercise is to empty your mind.

- Do not number the items because they need to pop out like free associations. Take whatever surfaces.
- Write only one item per line. No need to write the trigger words from the Trigger List. Use the triggers to free-associate to other incompletes.
- Begin by imagining yourself in your office, at home, or the place where bills and paperwork pile up. Those papers probably suggest incompletes. Begin writing, 1 item per line, what the papers represent. Then consider the material inside the drawers.
- When you finish a page or 20 minutes, stop, reward yourself, and take a 5 to 10 minutes break. This process may not feel like fun, yet it represents a high leverage activity you can do to organize and increase your productivity.
- If writing incompletes by yourself challenges you emotionally, ask a friend to read the Trigger List and write as you speak. Allow 20 to 40 minutes to generate the list.

How do you feel after writing down so many of the incompletes in your life? Most people feel drained after creating 4 to 6 pages of incompletes. Guess what? You feel drained and overwhelmed whether or not you create the list. This is the point! The "overwhelm" epitomizes energy you expend in worrying, feeling guilty, and mentally recycling your incompletes. When your energy drains, you feel tired and stuck; then you procrastinate. Incompletes spin in your mind like clothes in a dryer.

After listing pages of incompletes, people often say they feel light-headed. Exactly, you lighten your head by evicting your energy robbers. There may not be much left in your mind. Congratulations! You have just begun the process of reclaiming your energy!

What purpose does the mind serve if not to provide a storage container for incompletes? We believe minds inspire, receive from other dimensions, focus in the present as we communicate with people, interact with the environment, and finally, spawn creativity. Full, cluttered minds have little room for possibilities, the source of creativity. Trust your computers and time management systems to store and retrieve information.

Now review your List of Incompletes from two perspectives. First, cross off anything you choose to LET GO. By letting go, you say farewell to that item and free that energy for action.

Sometimes I feel like a mosquito in a nudist camp.
I know what to do, I don't know where to start.
Author Unknown

Few people know what to do at first...
that's why the art of doing lies in the beginning.
David Seabury

If the river flows clearly and cleanly
through the proper channel,
all will be well along the banks.
Brian Walker
Hua Hu Ching: The Unknown Teachings of Lao Tzu

We must remember to take action
along the basic lines and seams of the day.
Deng Ming-Dao
Tao

Review your Master List of Incompletes and identify your Moldy Oldies, those long overdue items. You know them.

> Rob kept a stack of *Time* magazines by his bed. He bought them, he felt he *should* read them, so he saved them for when he could find time to go through the pile. AND the pile kept growing. Finally, he decided to let go of all except the current issues. He made a rule to keep only the last two weeks'. Eventually he admitted to himself that he had ordered too many magazines, so he cut back on his subscriptions, his costs, and his guilt.

Keep the list nearby, and in the next few weeks, continue to add items as they pop into your mind, ones you overlooked at the time you created the list. Make your objective to commit every incomplete to the Master List. Once your list contains at least 95 percent of your incompletes, hone them into Next Action Steps.

Next Action Steps

A Next Action Step is **the very next step** to make progress with your incompletes. Next-Action-Step thinking cracks the procrastination that comes from feeling overwhelmed at the prospect of getting started.

Only a handful of acceptable Next Action Steps words exist, and, of course, they relate to the cycle of productivity:

- Write (copy, type, send, mail)
- Call (speak to, talk to)
- Schedule (read, file, organize)
- Think about
- Go to

Your Incomplete List contains this item—*Buy a new suit. Buy* is not a legitimate Next Action Step. By converting the incomplete into one of the Action Steps, it reads—*Go to clothing store.* You have not finished. Which store do you plan to go to first? If you do not know, will you visit a mall in search of a store? Reduce the action until it becomes one of the verbs listed above. You might write as your Next Action Step—*Go to Nordstrom at Tysons Mall.*

Assume you have a long overdue dental checkup on your list. The obvious Next Action Step would be to call the dentist. However, you realize you no longer have the dentist's number because you had your last checkup a long time ago. You remember Sharon has it, but Sharon has just moved. Cheryl knows where Sharon lives. Make *Calling Cheryl* your Next Action Step to get to the dentist.

WAYS I LIKE TO ACKNOWLEDGE MYSELF

MENTAL (*e.g.*, crossword puzzles, meaningful conversation with a friend, creative problem-solving, chess, spiritual insights)

EMOTIONAL (*e.g.*, listening to music, singing, watching children playing in a playground, deep belly laughing)

PHYSICAL (*e.g.*, aerobics, bubble bath, massage, soft clothing, hugging, sports)

NEW IDEAS:

See how specific you need to be? Keep questioning yourself to get to the Next Action Step you need to take to make progress.

Pretend you need to organize your office. Your thoughts:

1. What Next Action Step do I plan to take?
   File papers
2. What is the Next Step towards doing that?
   Sort papers
3. What is the Next Step to sorting the papers?
   Establish criteria for what to keep and what to toss
4. How long will it take to define criteria?
   About 15 minutes

My Next Action Step reads: *Schedule 15 minutes to establish criteria*. Then, schedule another chunk of time to begin sorting, and you have begun to tackle this noxious task.

We identified office organization as a Project because it contains many steps. As you go through your List of Incompletes, create two separate lists, Next Action Steps and Projects. Because every Project has a Next Action Step, your Next Action Step list will be longer than your Project list. Not every Action Step, however, is part of a project.

When you have separated your first page of incompletes into Projects and Next Action Steps, STOP! Reward yourself. You probably now feel organized as you never have before. Take the page of incompletes, crumple it, and throw it away. As you toss it, be aware of how you feel. Your feeling represents your experience of taking charge of your Incompletion List. Do you feel light? Free? At ease? Flowing? Accomplished? Get in touch with your feelings; expect to feel them many times during this process.

People who achieve results when they want, have about three-fourths of a page of active Projects, about 80 percent of which arise out of their annual goals. When you can see all your Projects in one place, you can easily set limits and say "No" to new ones.

The Next Step for you now: *Prioritize list of Next Action Steps*. Do not prioritize the Project List. Why?

Pretend you have two Projects:

A. *Sell bicycle.* You need space in your condo, and you want money. This Project of several steps feels easy for you.

B. *Plan family reunion.* The family wants a reunion this summer (5 months away). Many, many steps need to be taken to complete this Project. You feel overwhelmed at the complexity and difficulty of the project, without even knowing all the steps involved.

WAYS TO BE ACKNOWLEDGED AT WORK

- Time Off (*e.g.*, one day for special effort)
- Coupon discount book with community businesses
- Recognition from others
- Verbal thank you and appreciation
- Certificate for the wall (appreciation certificate)
- Written notes (*e.g.*, a job well done)
- Customers/clients/patients say nice things to me
- Annual increase based on performance review
- Periodic bonuses for excellent work on required tasks
- Periodic bonuses for special projects, extra effort
- Annual bonus
- Company profit shares
- Retirement plan contribution
- Surprise bonus
- Easily accessible parking space
- Mental health day
- Opportunities for future positions
- Money for training, professional growth, education, courses
- Time off for training, professional growth etc.
- Increased responsibility
- Annual gathering with no business agenda, *e.g.*, picnic
- Lunch with the boss
- Lunch as a group (the whole office)
- Article or interview in the company newsletter
- Symbolic gift representing Employee of the Month/Year

Dr. John Collings contributed many of these from his consulting.

You identify these Next Action Steps: *Project A. Schedule 10 minutes to scan paper for bike ad samples,* so that you can write one and *Project B. Call Aunt Jevene for addresses.*

If you only look at the project level, you would likely jump right in, perusing the paper and maybe even finding an ad for someone who wants to buy a bike like yours. Next thing you know, you might make an appointment for the person to test drive your bike, only to discover the tires need air. This step takes all day, and another day goes by with no progress on the reunion. Had you prioritized your Next Action Steps, you would have put the reunion first, so you would have called Aunt Jevene before searching for bike ads.

If you get new information in the middle of Project A, it might alter your priorities for the next step in Project A. For instance, if Aunt Jevene tells you that Cousin Joe's son would love to have a bike, you might cancel your plans to advertise the bike. By operating with prioritized Next Action Steps, you move within the Projects. This method permits you to work with comparable items. For how to prioritize, refer to Alan Lakein's book, **How To Get Control of Your Time and Your Life**, a Golden Oldie.

Now, take the final step, and perhaps the most important in the cycle of productivity: Acknowledge yourself. Taking this step impacts your well-being. As a recovering workaholic, I am all too familiar with attempting to do more, faster. I have learned that sometimes efficiency takes a back seat to effectiveness. Nowadays, I frequently do less than before in order to nurture my well-being. I choose my activities purposefully. My choices must provide me with doing **and** well-being. Accuse me of "wasting time" if you measure my productivity solely by what I do. But know that I feel fine paying attention to my well-being.

> In her business, Nel often receives four checks a day. She loves depositing them. So, every day she drives to the bank to deposit checks. Ed saves all of his for one weekend deposit. She takes more time, yet she nourishes her well-being.

How do you like to be acknowledged? Complete the Plurksheet on Self-Acknowledgment (See page 120). Notice how feeling acknowledged affects your creativity. Build acknowledgment into your plans, including your business planning process.

3. Workplace Acknowledgment
Management sometimes makes the error of assuming em-

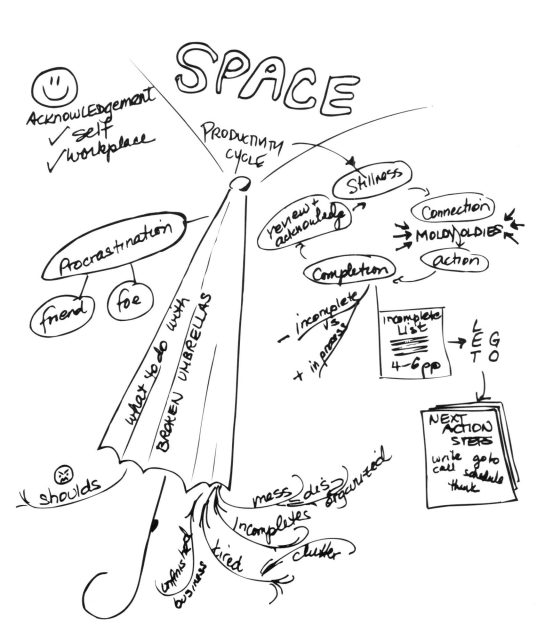

SPACE

:) Acknowledgement
✓ self
✓ workplace

Productivity Cycle

Stillness

renew + acknowledge

Completion

Connection

MOLDY OLDIES

Action

– incomplete vs
+ in process

Incomplete List
4-6 pp

L E G T O

Procrastination

friend   foe

what to do with
BROKEN UMBRELLAS

✓ shoulds

NEXT ACTION STEPS
write go to
call   schedule
think

mess   dis?   organized
Incompletes
unfinished business   tired   clutter

ployees only want money as acknowledgment. Many meaningful ways exist besides bonuses and raises. In workshops I ask employees to brainstorm acknowledgment ideas.

> At a healthcare organization, we polled the staff for what form of acknowledgment they most wanted. They responded, "If only the physicians would say *please* and *thank you*." At another facility, the staff requested a parking space near the building so they would feel safe when they left at night.

Read the collection of suggestions. How would you appreciate receiving praise in the workplace? If you manage others, ask your employees. If you have a manager, let him/her know.

We include self-acknowledgment and workplace acknowledgment as key components in the productivity cycle. Unless you feel affirmed for what you do, why bother doing!

LIST OF BRIEF SOLUTIONS for Chapter 7

1. The Productivity Cycle
2. Mental Spring Cleaning
3. Workplace Acknowledgment

ACTION

How do I intend to apply these solutions to my life to get the results I want?

What Next Action Step do I plan to take?

The Incompletion List deals mostly with broken umbrellas of our physical environment. We also have incompletes, sometimes even Moldy Oldies, in our people networks. To learn how to sort through your relationships and prune away those who do not support you to have sufficient time for those who do, read Chapter 8, **Prune Your People Inventory**.

SIMPLY LIVE IT UP

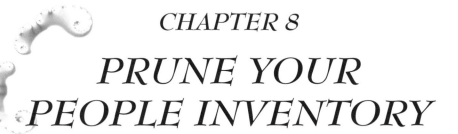

CHAPTER 8
PRUNE YOUR PEOPLE INVENTORY

People, people everywhere;
no more room for me.

Teri-E Belf

I need my space.
Bryan Bowles

The only man who is really free
is the one who can turn down an invitation to dinner
without giving an excuse.
Jules Renard

Acquaintances are like magazine subscriptions.
John I. Smith

Just say NO

CHAPTER 8

PRUNE YOUR PEOPLE INVENTORY

PROBLEM

As an extrovert, I don't have time to see all my friends.
I have outgrown some of my friends, but I don't know how to tactfully stop accepting invitations.
I can't say "No" without feeling guilty when people ask me to do something for them.
I don't have enough time for myself. No vacancy!

This exploration may be hazardous to your status quo.

WHAT IF . . . ?

- I took time to maintain, revitalize, and strengthen the friendships and relationships I treasured
- I let go of those people who no longer support me
- I spent time with my family
- I stayed current with long distance correspondence
- I easily said "No" without feeling guilty

THEN . . .

I would have a new option for protecting myself by saying "No" to people I do not want to spend time with. I would simplify my life by maintaining only a support network of people I choose.

SIMPLY

This chapter describes how to take an inventory of people currently in your life to decide whom to keep as part of your support network, whom to let go, and whom to add. This process, called *pruning*, contains eleven steps.

Why prune your people inventory? Many extroverts try to spend quality time with a long list of people which actually takes time or steals time from their dearest, not to mention their sleep time, Plurk time, and quiet time. If you reach out to people, you attract

Simplify, simplify.
Henry David Thoreau
Walden

SIMPLY LIVE IT UP

them like a human magnet. You may have solutions to downsize things other than people. If you have too many shirts, you could donate or consign them. If you have too much money, you could contribute it or call us. Too much paperwork? Buy another file cabinet. Do you have so many people you "don't know what to do"? What criteria do you have for downsizing your people inventory?

Many middle-aged women take on innumerable giving roles because their role models gave continually—to PTA, church, community, and us. It felt selfish to give to oneself. Many women did not know how to receive or even what they wanted to receive. They had few role models for balancing giving and receiving. Many chose social work, teaching, or nursing—careers of giving, giving, giving.

You only have a finite amount of energy. Once you deplete your energy by giving it away, you collapse. To bring receiving into alignment, create the space to receive from others. Next, give to yourself. Adopt the attitude, "It's okay for me to let go of feeling selfish and accept the attitude of self-caring." By granting yourself permission to prune your people inventory, you create space to give to your highest valued people and to yourself.

LIVE IT

Maintaining contact with too many people can burden even extroverts. Saying "Yes" to people who request your time when you would rather say "No" drains extroverts and introverts. We may be reluctant to say "No" because we fear hurting feelings, theirs or ours. If you decline several invitations with the hope that the caller will interpret the "real" message, dread returning phone calls, say you are busy or find some other "socially acceptable" excuse, you succeed only in delaying the requested encounter. You run the risk of hampering your well-being by feeling guilty and annoyed at your dishonesty in telling "little white lies."

Pruning your people inventory gives you practice in speaking with integrity, tact, courage, and clarity, and freedom from guilt when you need to say "No." Pruning works best if you have a strong value in being honest with yourself and preserving your well-being. You can create synergy between your people inventory and your values, priorities, and purpose.

UP

Revisit why you have particular relationships in your life. Few people have an awareness of all the people in their network and

PRUNE YOUR PEOPLE INVENTORY: MASTER LIST

<u>People</u>   <u>Value Received</u>   <u>Current Importance</u>   <u>Future Learning</u>

the type of support they receive from each. Having a grasp of the big picture enables you to make purposeful choices.

Prune to clear space for yourself and special others. Having space gives you quiet time to reflect, gain perspective on your life situation, and nurture your spirit.

BRIEF SOLUTION: Prune Your People Inventory

1. Create a master list of all the people in your life. Be sure to include close and casual friends (though you may not have written to them nor seen them for a long time), intimate relationships, and acquaintances. People who occupy your mind, even infrequently, remain in your life. Do not forget family, relatives, colleagues, and business contacts, former and present. Include all the community, spiritual, educational, and professional organizations to which you belong. If you have moved, you may find that you have collected "people inventories" in several cities and countries.

2. Reflect on the value you have received from knowing each person. Recalling specifics, pictograph what experiences had value for you, and write a script from your ideas. The pictograph may tap into your other-than-conscious mind and surface your true beliefs without justification or excuses.

3. Consider what value and learning is still possible if the relationship continues? Add to your notes or pictograph. Think about how many minutes, hours, days you require for the relationship to continue at its present level. Ask yourself if you choose to put in the amount of time and effort relative to the value (benefit) you receive. Consider how much time it might take to strengthen or deepen the connection during the next year.

4. Select those people you choose to prune. Do you have any people Moldy Oldies? Can you "let go" of them to create space in your life for those you want to keep or add, or for yourself? On an index card, put the name of each person you decide to prune along with the pictograph and the script.

5. Clarify why you elect to delete this person from your inventory (What did you give to the relationship, what did you gain, what do you want to give, and what do you currently receive). Consider the situation from your external point of view as well as internal state.

Rita had known John for five years. They did things together eight to ten times a year and often saw each other at professional meetings. John told the truth about his life. He initiated getting together. He shared Rita's love for adventure, exotic dining, and dancing. He taught her effective ways to use her new computer.

Rita began to notice that she was giving much more than she was getting from the relationship. She felt the burden of being John's social worker. She was ready to give that up. Instead she wanted people in her life who had a great degree of self-esteem, instead of always asking for help in solving problems. John had told Rita that she was one of the few positive persons in his life. As long as he had her around, he had no motivation to broaden his base of friendships or seek professional psychological help.

Rita provided the lightness and fun. John was so serious. Rita listened to his problems and practiced creative problem-solving. She challenged his ideas. She loved the adventures they took. Once she had felt valued and needed, but currently she was not getting much except a knot in her stomach each time she said "Yes" when John called when she would have rather said "No."

"John, I have too many people in my life right now. I need to focus and select those people who can keep me moving on the track I have set for myself. I want to let you know directly that I will not be spending time with you in the future. I value our friendship and I have grown from it. I am a much better problem-solver since I met you. I have learned many new dance steps, and I can finally use my computer. I have valued our friendship. However, I am clear that I want more time for those things that are directly aligned with my future goals. My needs are to socialize within a group that is in harmony with my future. I will treasure the wonderful memories of our time together."

6. Write a script for your face-to-face meeting. Select one person, and plan your conversation. Select an easy pruning for your first one, so you can experience a success. Tap into your emotionally neutral space as you write your script.

7. Schedule private, uninterrupted time. Planning it face to face allows you to pay attention to the subtleties and innuendos of the verbal and body communication. Remember, you intend to let the person know you received value from the connection even though you choose to close the relationship. Prepare a script for the next time he/she calls you or you unexpectedly meet. Regardless of who initiates the meeting, you must take charge of your scenario.

8. Rehearse your part of the conversation. Anticipate nonverbal and verbal responses. Imagine the worst scenario, and prepare your responses from your emotional neutrality and your highest values.

9. Have the conversation. Share what aspects of the relationship you have valued. Explain your people inventory goal and why you are saying "Good-bye" now.

10. Review what you learned from the experience? What did I do well? What might I have done? Add to your pictograph.

11. Acknowledge yourself for taking the first step in pruning your people inventory, a major step to safeguard your valuable time, self-esteem, and well-being.

When your support network reflects people you choose, step back and examine your new network:
- How did I bring these people into my network?
- What areas are missing people?
- Do I have alternative support if something happens to one person who serves many roles?

You intend your communication to enhance self-esteem rather than to diminish it. Completion means that **you** feel good because you honestly have expressed yourself and your needs. You have taken care of yourself in a self-caring way.

Congratulations. By taking charge of your people inventory, you fashion your destiny, and become a role model for others to review their own people inventories.

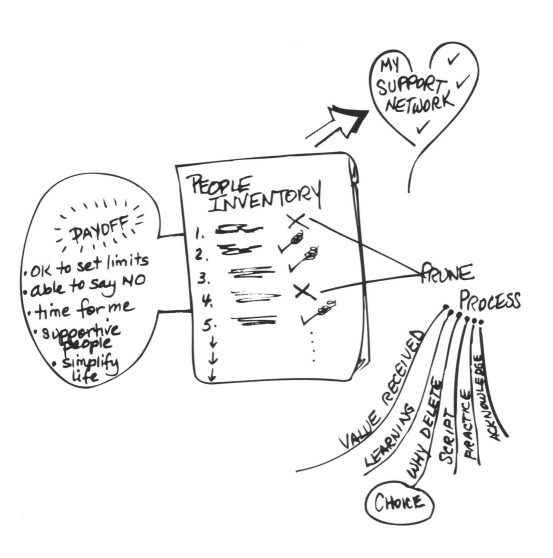

BRIEF SOLUTION for Chapter 8: Prune Your People Inventory

STEPS
1. Create a master list of all the people in your life
2. Reflect on the value you have received from knowing each person
3. Consider what the relationship holds for value and learning
4. Select those people you choose to prune
5. Write a script for your face-to-face meeting
6. Clarify why you elect to delete this person from your inventory
7. Schedule private, uninterrupted time
8. Rehearse your part of the conversation
9. Have the conversation
10. Review what you learned from the experience
11. Acknowledge yourself for taking the first step

ACTION

How do I intend to apply this solution to my life to get the results I want?

What Next Action Step do I plan to take?

Even if you cannot design your destiny, learn from the glitches, re-energize your vital spark, play the Results and Well-Being Games, compile Guidelines for Winning, transform your relationship with time, design your Ideal Week, throw out the broken umbrellas, prune your people network, you can still learn about **Plurking**. Plurking is SIMPLY playing while you work. The following chapter is required reading.

SIMPLY LIVE IT UP

CHAPTER 9
PLURKING

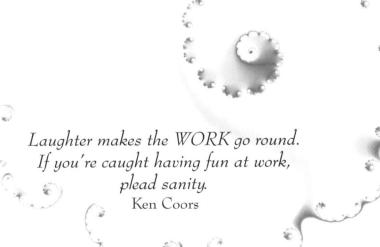

Laughter makes the WORK go round.
If you're caught having fun at work,
plead sanity.
Ken Coors

The dolphin as a master of games
behaves as if there is no competition,
no loser, no winners,
only fun for all.
Author Unknown

Allowing joy to come forward in one's work
frees the creative mind,
reduces stress,
and is wonderfully infectious.
Gary Iredell

CHAPTER 9

PLURKING

PROBLEM

I just don't allow myself to have fun anymore.
I'm not even sure what fun means to me.
I work at having fun.
Fun at work? You've got to be kidding!

When hearts are high the time will fly, so whistle while you work.
Snow White and the Seven Dwarfs

WHAT IF . . . ?

- Going to work felt like fun
- Others like to spend time with me because I have fun
- Living is fun instead of hard work

THEN . . .

How different my life would be if I found fun in all I did. My tasks and chores would feel like fun. Fun would appear as easy as blinking. My license plate would read like Tina's: FUN-NE1?

SIMPLY

This chapter introduces a collection of the authors' techniques for decorating your life with fun—plurking, playing while you clean your desk (chore plurk), playing with words (word plurk), playing while you handle the paperwork (paper plurk), and silent singing.

LIVE IT

When you are having fun, instead of feeling guilty for shirking—Plurk!—Play while you work, and increase your job productivity, career happiness, creativity, and energy.

UP

Play lightens your energy. When you Plurk, you SIMPLY LIVE IT

More important than talent, strength, or knowledge
is the ability to laugh at yourself
and enjoy the pursuit of your dreams.
Amy Grant

Fun is a biochemical brain state.
Llyle Palmer, Ph.D.

Some people talk about play
as if it were a relief from serious business,
but for children play is serious business....
Fred Rogers, of Mr. Roger's Neighborhood

UP!

BRIEF SOLUTIONS

Serious people walk around with blinders. With your nose to the grindstone, you close yourself to outside stimuli. People with a plurkful attitude behave flexibly, expecting newness and creativity to spark at any moment. Plurkers delight to share possibilities and ideas. Adopt playful ideas for anything that feels like work to you, such as shopping, cleaning house, and writing reports.

1. Plurking

Over twenty years ago I observed that most people did not have fun at work, even on a good day with minimal stress. They waited for the weekend to have fun. So I made UP a word to integrate the two seemingly foreign ideas, play and work. I created the word *PLURK* to mean "play while you work," and I have been using it and passing out "Ask me how I PLURK" buttons ever since.

> I used to manage a training and development department in a prestigious healthcare organization. We had lots of fun at work. During one of our Management Development seminars, a surgeon asked me about my Plurk button. I explained that it meant "play while you work." He responded with great seriousness, "Maybe you can play in the Training Department; in Surgery we deal with life and death. " All I could say was, "I thought healthcare was a matter of life!" I made my point, and he lightened UP considerably.

Michael Jones, accomplished composer and pianist, notes we refer to *playing* piano, not *working* piano. In what other fields can we Plurk? In your next staff meeting ask, "How can we Plurk today?" Brainstorm ideas and implement them.

2. Chore Plurk

> Grocery Shopping
> As a single parent, I felt that grocery shopping kept me from having time with my son. To Plurk, I created a game. We split the shopping list and raced to see who could bring items to the register first. A bonus—a decrease in impulse buying.

When you delight in the game,
the effort seems unimportant.
Author Unknown

The future does not belong to the meek or the rigid,
but to the nimble.
Author Unknown

It is not whether you win or lose,
it is how you play the game.
Author Unknown

Say!
I like green eggs and ham!
I do! I like them, Sam-I-am!
Dr. Seuss
Green Eggs and Ham

SIMPLY LIVE IT UP

The word *chore* connotes drudgery. You can Plurk anywhere, any time. Use daily tasks to activate your imagination.

House Cleaning

Turn house cleaning into fun. Play a John Phillip Sousa march to keep yourself moving. Pretend you have to finish dusting the living room before certain parts finish. Turn UP the volume so you don't hear the phone and risk interruptions.

> Doing Dishes
> I guided a woman who disliked doing dishes into an experience she truly enjoyed. I encouraged her to appreciate the beauty of hot water interacting with a greasy plate.

Sometimes Plurking means slowing down to savor moments. Have you ever noticed the beautiful prism of light created by droplets of water as they glide through grease? Can you imagine soap bubble prisms transforming your dish duty?

> Preparing Meals
> Charlotte used to keep a half-acre organic garden. By romping out to the field, she and her children could pick their own menus. They munched corn-on-the-cob, tomatoes, cucumbers, green beans, peas, lettuce, even okra—fresh food and no dishes!

3. Word Plurk

Tumbling with words keeps us in Plurking mode. As the sole proprietors of our words, we command our Plurk allies. Pictograph the words you Plurk. When you become playful and friendly with words, you will find rich humor and wisdom popping in and. . . out, and. . . UP. Let us know what Plurk words you create.

> At a gathering of my coaching consultants, we created our own vocabulary. For example, *unthinging* became the designated word describing eradicating unnecessary things in life. We adopted the phrase *very great* as a way of emphasizing our appreciation. Throughout the gathering we had fun saying and hearing *unthinging* and *very great*.

4. Silent Singing

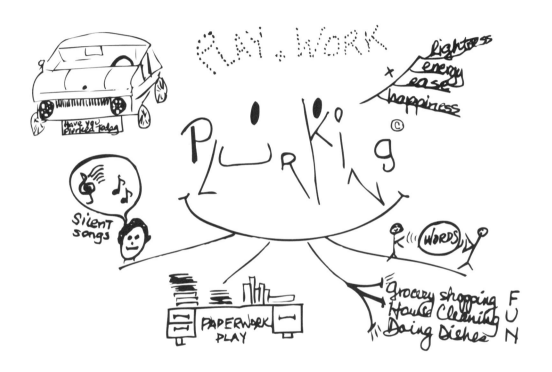

4. Silent Singing

Which songs boost you UP to new levels of lightness?

> I love the Disney movie *Snow White and the Seven Dwarfs*. When I encounter a difficult work situation, I burst into my silent singing coping mechanism, "Whistle While You Work." I got through my divorce singing to myself, "When You Walk Through a Storm, Hold Your Head Up High," from the play *Carousel*. Now I can whistle and hold my head up any time.

Another new bumper sticker: Have you Plurked today?

LIST OF BRIEF SOLUTIONS for Chapter 9

1. Plurking
2. Chore Plurk
3. Word Plurk
4. Silent Singing

ACTION

How do I intend to apply these solutions to my life to get the results I want?

What Next Action Step do I plan to take?

Plurking involves participation by the whole of you. If one of your incompletes deals with reading, "plearn" with the amazing system for Plurking while you read: **The Information-Age Learning Process**.

THE
INFORMATION-AGE
LEARNING
PROCESS

Be patient with all that is unresolved in your heart
And try to love the questions themselves
Do not seek for the answers that cannot be given
For you would not be able to live them
And the point is to live everything
Live the questions now
And perhaps without knowing it
You will live along some day into the answers.
Rainer Maria Rilke

Ready, Set, Learn!
Teri-E Belf

Desperation to know gets in the way of knowing.
Charlotte Ward

If you are not living on the edge,
you take up too much room.
Native American saying

Creation already exists. We are merely formatting it.
Teri-E Belf

CHAPTER 10

THE INFORMATION-AGE LEARNING PROCESS

PROBLEM

I feel like a casualty of the Information Age. Information is multiplying exponentially, and I'm drowning on the Internet. Help!

> *Anything can be achieved in small deliberate steps.*
> *But there are times you need the courage*
> *to take a great leap;*
> *you can't cross a chasm in two small jumps.*
> David Lloyd George

WHAT IF ... ?

- I capitalized on my intuitive intelligence
- I gave myself permission to say I don't know
- I asked questions about everything
- I admitted that I will never know everything
- I gave UP being perfect

THEN ...

I would process information masterfully. I would feel vitally energetic and well-informed. I would relish learning and creating. My investments of time, energy, and money would compensate me with a rich diversity of experiences. I would consider my life as one big learning opportunity.

SIMPLY

Life presents us with myriad learning opportunities. We have, in this country, already arrived in the Information Age. Once the operative word *computer* overtook *typewriter*, we heard our bookshelves and in-boxes groaning. More to learn calls for ingenious human technology, which, fortunately, we already possess in our pro-

HOLOGRAM

Energy

THE BIG PICTURE

DO BE

Inhabit Health	Universe
Impassion Yourself	Galaxy
Investigate Your Impulse	Solar System
Imagine	Earth
Intake	Human
Integrate	I
Inquire	Neurotransmitter
Identify	Atom
Interpret	Electron
Interact	Quark

details

Energy

digious brains and supple bodies. We present here a way to learn on purpose by transmuting strategic questions into answers quickly and easily on your own terms.

LIVE IT

We learn best when we have fun learning, when we dream UP answers, then analyze, judge, and act on them, when we feed the mind a question and project results, when we involve the whole brain, not just the word-loving, decision-making neocortex. By following brief, effective strategies, you can proceed with deceptive ease, while rendering phenomenal results.

Coordinate both hemispheres—your creative mind, which gathers and stores ideas at many thousands of pieces of information a minute and responds with creative insights; and your logical mind, which analyzes and judges the stored information. The process leads you in a deductive pattern—from macro-questions to micro-questions, from theory to specifics, from macro-answers to micro-answers, from concept to fact, until you get the amount of detail you want.

As you engage your inner mind in a contemplative, private space, you enter a zone of rapport with information. Consciously choosing the brain-wave state to match each step of the process, your body and mind can form a partnership to discover answers to your important questions.

UP

The Information-Age Learning Process creates a quietly focused mind—prerequisite for learning. This state allows you to Intake vast amounts of information to shed light on your issues, helping you make good decisions, reduce stress, and feel good, too. Even as it increases concentration, the process simultaneously introduces a sense of order and control. If you expand your belief in what the human mind can do, and if you expect to get results, you can develop yourself, manage your time, realize your mental prowess, and experience spirituality associated with your intellect. When in doubt on how to proceed, ask the question: What road leads to learning?

BRIEF SOLUTION: The Information-Age Learning Process

When we learn, we go through a patterned response to something that appeals to us. Life on earth learns, particularly humans, who consider learning their manifest destiny. Even though the learning process is the stuff of life, it seems to be a very complex function,

In a test of Janusian thinking ["actively conceiving two or more opposites or antitheses simultaneously during the course of the creative process"] *Arthur Rothenberg, Clinical Professor of Psychiatry at Harvard Medical School, administered timed word-association tests to twelve Nobel laureates, eighteen hospitalized patients, and 113 college students divided into categories of high and low creativity. The Nobel laureates gave the highest proportion of opposite (unusual) responses. They also furnished these opposite responses at significantly faster rates than common responses. Indeed, their average speed of opposite response was fast enough to indicate that conceptualizing the opposites could have been simultaneous. Rothenberg thinks of these highly creative people as engaging in a "translogical process."*

Richard M. Restak, M.D.
The Modular Brain

*At about the age of nine I decided
never to believe anything because it was convenient.
I began reversing every statement to see
if the opposite was also true....
As soon as you put a "not" into an assertion,
a whole range of other possibilities opens out....*

Keith Johnstone
Impro: Improvisation and the Theatre

because most people, at one time or another, protest change, clinging to what they already know, yet complaining miserably when they are not learning, railing against boredom and wasting time. What factors throw us into such a double bind, and can we learn to conquer them? How can we acknowledge our fear of failure and triumph with the love of learning?

1. One to the Power of Ten

• **Inhabit Health:** Get plenty of sleep, good food, water, and exercise, and translate glitches into opportunities.

• **Impassion Yourself:** Scan the world for learning opportunities. Stay at the ready for the new and different.

• **Investigate Your Impulse:** Noticing what is different indicates you have something to learn. When you feel an immediate attraction to being and doing something, you have just recognized an Information-Age learning opportunity.

• **Imagine:** See, hear, and feel yourself doing and being whatever attracts you. In your imagination, dare to do anything. This step can ignite your desire and build motivation to propel you toward a new result.

• **Intake:** Gather information, but make no judgment at this point. Stay alert for anyone or anything that contributes. With your reticular system beamed on a particular learning opportunity, information will appear as if by magic; and the more, the better.

When you first use the Information-Age process, you may be tempted to analyze and make choices during Intake because it feels as if nothing is happening, which usually disconcerts a neophyte. But, paradoxically, what goes in through non-conscious channels may delay satisfaction or consciously knowing the meaning or what action to take. However, during the crucial step of Intake, the mind does store the whole experience in order to Integrate and Identify it later. **Intake ensures that the next steps will work.**

• **Integrate:** Tell your more-than-conscious mind you wish to Integrate the information in the hours to come. Pose questions to yourself about what you have been investigating. Although it may sound silly, when you talk to yourself or ask questions of your more-than-conscious mind, speak politely, as if to a loved one, which, in-

Rebecca: *I never told you about that letter Jane Crofut got from her minister when she was sick. He wrote Jane a letter and on the envelope the address was like this: It said: Jane Crofut. The Crofut Farm; Grover's Corners; Sutton County; New Hampshire; United States of America.*

George: *What's funny about that?*

Rebecca: *But listen, it's not finished: The United States of America; Continent of North America; Western Hemisphere; the Earth; the Solar System; the Universe; the Mind of God—that's what it said on the envelope.*

George: *What do you know!*

Rebecca: *And the postman brought it just the same.*

George: *What do you know!*

Thornton Wilder
Our Town, Act I

deed, your Self is.

Your brain is bound to automatically Integrate information you have taken in. Ideally, allow 24 hours including the four to five REM periods during an eight-hour sleep, before you begin to Identify on a conscious level what you have learned. The dawn dreams often surface to Theta consciousness at least enough to tantalize us. In order to use them, capture their wisdom in your preferred way— on NightLights, pictograph, tape recorder, or dream journal (See Chapter 12).

During REM sleep, the brain patterns data, saving new over existing information, much as we update data on a computer. Dreams add the day's news, preparing us to cope with new existential issues and to problem-solve ancient and recent challenges in life.

• **Inquire:** Next, take a few minutes to form questions. What are you curious about? What do you guess might be the main idea or lesson to learn? Child and master alike learn by going into an intensely motivated state directed by purpose and fueled by questions. When you frame your interest as questions about a learning experience, before or after Intake, you call your whole body to join the search party for answers and to celebrate in the ultimate *aha's*. Thinking with a question in mind and discovering the answer feels wonderful, probably because it actually causes your brain to grow.

Pinpointing where on the hierarchy of information you want to enter the equation can speed your learning and creativity. With deductive reasoning we aim high for a big payoff: Often, if you understand the formula or overarching idea, you can easily access the example. The bigger the picture, the more information carried. However, for paradox, consider the hologram. Like the Julia set, which repeats infinitely, ideas that form a whole appear also whole within themselves. Learning from specific to general seems to require extra effort, so to be brief, conserve time and energy by proceeding from the broad concept to the level of detail that satisfies your questions.

If you ask macro-questions, you will likely notice concepts, theories, or major themes. A macro-answer contains a vast potential of smaller answers within its domain. If you seek a detail, then for efficiency, begin asking questions at the detail level.

Generate questions on a systematic basis by noting the "icons"—the important people, events, and contexts that make up the learning experience. Pictograph each icon as you hopscotch through the learning experience, recording questions around each one. When you have enough questions, hop to your next step.

It would be a little like trying to pin down the note in a piece of music [that] is the carrier of the emotional meaning of the piece. Of course there is no such note, because the emotional meaning is carried on a very high level, by large "chunks" of the piece, not by single notes.
Eric Hofstadter
Gödel, Escher, Bach

We practice the wisdom of prevention by seeing our actions in perspective, looking to the larger cycles.
Diane Dreher
The TAO of Inner Peace

- **Identify:** Begin to Identify answers to your questions about the learning experience. Pictograph your *aha's* until you have answered your questions or until you feel finished, whichever comes first. Consciously analyze any portions of the learning you want to. Remember to savor good feelings of growth and resolution.

- **Interpret:** Make the learning your own. Adapt the information to your uses, and put your imprint on it, for learning naturally flowers into creativity, the payoff of consciousness.

- **Interact**: Use what you have created. As you Interact with people and systems in your world, assess and adjust what you have learned, pass along your answers, and discover new questions.

I describe asking and answering a set of questions as *tumbleweed learning*: we loop from question, through process, to answer, which, in turn, usually results in other questions, over and over again. The Information-Age learning process blows tumbleweeds before us faster and faster. We learn exponentially, thereby stimulating more questions, which, in turn, search for answers. How will you use your recent realizations? How will the *aha's* make a difference in your life? What did your *aha's* resolve? What other questions are now forming in your searching mind? ??   ????

2. Emotions

- **Fear:** Fear and pain, two powerful reticular system basic instincts designed to save our lives, can hamper learning. After you catch your breath, honor your emotion, then use it to discover the flip side. Ask yourself, "What do I fear?" and "Is fear warranted in this situation?" If you answer "Failure" and "No," perhaps your fear points to a learning opportunity.

> "What do I do when I'm down? I review how far I've come since last year. I set weekly and monthly goals, achievable goals, not impossibly high ones. Then, if I don't get them one week, I get them in three. That's okay, as long as I'm growing. Sometimes I look in the mirror in the morning and feel it's going to be a heavy day." Bryan puts up posters of his sports heroes to inspire him. "I don't look to how they live the rest of their lives. I have my family for that. I admire them for how they excel in their sport. I have a poster of a body builder and one of a woman running in a cornfield; it looks as if she could run forever."

• **Confusion:** Confusion heralds learning. That mental state arises out of the neurotransmitter scramble to make new dendritic connections. So, strange as it may sound, when you feel your brow knitting, celebrate, and look for learning.

However, no matter how well you project, life brings unpredictable results. For that reason, many winners count persistence far, far above talent. Mental and physical toughness diminishes the difference between what you sometimes get—Glitches—and what you want—Results. Although you cannot predict what will happen, you certainly can control how you meet your challenges.

• **Joy:** As your foundation for living, you can choose joy at being alive and take opportunities to learn as they open ever before you.

3. Support: Engage mentors, coaches, and role models as metaphors for success. They give you a real life basis for visualization (See Chapter 2) and human support.

BRIEF SOLUTION for Chapter 10: The Information-Age Learning Process

STEPS
1. One to the Power of Ten
2. Emotions
3. Support

ACTION

How do I intend to apply this solution to my life to get the results I want?

What Next Action Step do I plan to take?

The Information-Age Learning Process suggests an approach for optimal learning consistent with our brain power. To apply this process to one of our best ways to learn, read Chapter 11, **The PhotoReading Whole Mind System.**

SIMPLY LIVE IT UP

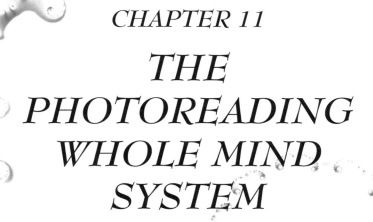

CHAPTER 11

THE PHOTOREADING WHOLE MIND SYSTEM

*Get your reading done
in the time you have
at the comprehension level you need.*

Paul Scheele

The road to knowledge begins with the turn of a page.
Chinese Fortune Cookie

Why are we reading, if not in hope of beauty laid bare, life heightened and its deepest mystery probed? Can the writer isolate and vivify all in experience that most deeply engages our intellects and our hearts? Can the writer renew our hope for literary forms? Why are we reading if not in hope that the writer will magnify and dramatize our days, will illuminate and inspire us with wisdom, courage, and the possibility of meaningfulness, and will press upon our minds the deepest mysteries, so that we may feel again their majesty and power?
Annie Dillard
The Writing Life

CHAPTER 11

THE PHOTOREADING WHOLE MIND SYSTEM

PROBLEM

I have too little time, too much to read, and too much stress.

At first people refuse to believe that a strange new thing
can be done, then they begin to hope it can't be done;
then they see it can be done—
then it is done
and all the world wonders why it was not done centuries before.
Francis Hodgson Burnett
The Secret Garden

WHAT IF . . . ?

- I selected to read what I wanted to know
- I asked questions that developed my interest in everything I should read
- I stated my purpose before I began reading—every time
- I trusted myself to comprehend a book at the speed my right brain saw the words—in minutes, not hours
- I actively projected meaning as I read

THEN . . .

I would establish a personal context of being a well-read, well-rested, vibrant participant in life. My investments of time, energy, and money in reading would fairly compensate me with a rich diversity of ideas. I would associate reading, not with pressure and guilt, but with pleasure and growth, and I would balance it with other activities in my schedule. I would dispense with perfection.

SIMPLY

Find answers to your questions by thinking, reading, and processing information quickly, easily, and intentionally with the

I tried to resist schooling, but I accepted the idea that my intelligence was the most important part of me. I tried to be clever in everything I did. The damage was greatest in areas where my interests and the school's seemed to coincide: in writing, for example (I wrote and rewrote, and lost all my fluency). I forgot that inspiration isn't intellectual, that you don't have to be perfect. In the end I was reluctant to attempt anything for fear of failure, and my first thoughts never seemed good enough. Everything had to be corrected and brought into line.

In one moment I knew that the valuing of men by their intelligence is crazy, that the peasants watching the night sky might feel more than I feel, that the man who dances might be superior to myself—word-bound and unable to dance. From then on I noticed how warped many people of great intelligence are, and I began to value people for their actions, rather than their thoughts.

Keith Johnstone
Impro: Improvisation and the Theatre

PhotoReading whole mind system, brain child of Paul Scheele.

The word *reading* has been defined in many ways, depending on the rate people have devised to publish their thoughts. The definition you use for *reading* predestines the quality of the information you absorb. Most people nowadays read at 225-250 words per minute, only a little faster than primary school students—good for newspaper headlines, letters and memos, and a vacation book a year. Some few fly through material at computer speed—extracting what they need from libraries of periodicals, trade journals, and books. We bear happy news: the way the human brain works, **what the few can do the many can learn.**

This system works on fiction as well as nonfiction, memos, letters, journals, and magazine articles. It follows a deductive pattern—from theory to specifics, from concept to fact, until you get the amount of detail you want. Details are important—but not every detail, not every word. In the first place, four to eleven percent of the words on the page carry the meaning; some words are suns, some cosmic dust. To be human, to be brilliant, to be brief is to differentiate what is important from what is not.

The computer ushered in the Information Age. Now we need to read at speeds comparable to how fast we can produce print.

LIVE IT

By following The PhotoReading whole mind system, you can enhance your learning and greatly reduce time you spend regular reading. You can automatically single out the information you value and mentally highlight those passages you want to savor. No longer does anyone have to settle for kindergarten slowness. We can easily bypass subvocalization, regression, and most forms of dyslexia. Using the appropriate hemisphere for each brief time through the material, you can program your creative mind to store meaning at the astonishing rate of 25,000 or more words a minute. Read like an impresario with the whole mind five-step process: Prepare, Preview, PhotoRead, Activate, and Rapid Read.

UP

Paradoxically, Whole Mind Reading relaxes as it increases concentration and promotes learning. The Alpha state (See page 38) serves as an ever-present resource for many activities besides reading. Experiment with it when you go to a meeting, play a game, visit with a friend, or learn a skill.

PARAPHERNALIA
FOR LEARNERS, DREAMERS, AND CREATORS

1. Your *sitio*, your place...............discover just the right cozy place for you
2. Window shades or drapes to create a dimly-lit atmosphere
3. Full-spectrum lighting with dimmer
4. Music box or system, with headset, voice-activated tape recorder
5. CD's and tapes, including Baroque, Classic, Romantic, New Age, and self-help, inspirational, and relaxation tapes
6. Eye pillow, neck pillow, chair pillow
7. Reading slant board
8. Soft afghan or comforter
9. Colored pens, large pad of paper, pen with night light or a separate small night light
10. Hydroculator or hot water bottle
11. Hot water or herbal tea in a specially chosen cup
12. Selection of reading material
13. A plant, fresh flowers, or incense
14. Answering machine and do-not-disturb button on telephone

OR

Internal focus wherever you are.

As the separate steps weave back and forth between left and right hemispheres, you balance your body-brain-mind and economize on mental effort and time. PhotoReading, the innovative center of the system, activates the creative side of your brain, which gets short shrift in many other aspects of our Western culture.

Fueled by your stated purpose, you can use this system to propel you toward your short- and long-term goals. It introduces a sense of order and control when you have too much to read and too little time. Because it works, whole mind reading saves hours that you can spend on reading more or enjoying other UP activities. You can even transform all your reading into pleasure reading.

BRIEF SOLUTION: The PhotoReading Whole Mind System

For for my master's thesis, I researched over 150 books to winnow my "Works Cited" to a hundred. As I stood in the stacks, I would first "get the feel" of a book in a dreamy way. After fanning the pages, I would start to browse wherever I happened to turn. Almost every time, I found an idea or a quote that exactly fitted my needs. When I thought about my process at all, I thought myself very lucky.

When Paul Scheele noticed the "right-brain" phenomenon of flipping through material and finding information "jumping off the page," he recognized it as a pattern.

Cut the Gordian Knot of too much to read and too little time. Apply the framework of The Information-Age Learning Process to any kind of reading. Before reading anything the regular way, flexibly Prepare, Preview, PhotoRead, Activate, Rapid Read:

1. Prepare: State your purpose for reading, then enter the ideal state.
   • Whole Mind Reading offers a system of flexible brief approaches to written materials led by your purpose. I have found that by stating my purpose in question form before I begin reading, and by refining and restating it every subsequent step, I call my whole body to join the search party for the answers and to celebrate the *aha's*. And once you know what you want, you can easily relax.
   • Settle yourself comfortably. Because reading involves thinking, rather than merely seeing, we need to prepare our body-mind to concentrate, which means ignoring distractions in the environment and focusing intently on the text. You can achieve the Alpha brain-wave state any time you want by doing a few simple

Most of the "real work," both in the acquisition of cognitive procedures and skills and in the execution of cognitive operations, such as encoding and interpretation of stimuli, is being done at the level to which our consciousness has no access.... The "responsibilities" of this inaccessible level of our cognition are not limited to the housekeeping operations, such as retrieving information from memory or adjusting the level of arousal; they are directly involved in the development of interpretive categories, drawing inferences, determining emotional reactions, and other high-level cognitive operations traditionally associated with consciously controlled thinking.

Pawel Lewicki, Thomas Hill, and Maria Czyzewska
"Nonconscious Acquisition of Information"
American Psychologist, June 1992

things. Breathe low in the abdomen, long, thoughtful, even breaths. Closing your eyes may help you focus within. In a bookstore or an office, without doing anything dramatic, I take a few deep breaths and relax from the top of my head to the tips of my toes. I may appear tired or mellow. Memorize this relaxed body feeling so that you can use it as a resource any time you choose. It can help you concentrate on any activity, not just reading.

2. Preview: This step includes a very brief survey, followed by finding a few trigger words every 15 to 20 pages to determine the thesis, or gist, and whether you can get what you need from this source. If the answer is "No," choose another source; if "Yes," refine your purpose questions and proceed to the next step. The preview is the oldest and briefest of the accelerated reading techniques; take 1 to 5 minutes for an article, 5 to 8 minutes for a book. Great readers project what the author is going to conclude; then, as they read, they weigh the ideas they encounter against what they guessed. In that way, they confirm what they know, and learn the new.

　• Begin previewing by surveying the text: the title, author, copyright page or paragraph, table of contents, chapter or section titles, beginning and end paragraphs or pages. For nonfiction, state or pictograph the gist; for fiction, look for names of characters, locales, dates, and a general sense of the action or conflict.

　• Trigger words, words that stand out on the page, indicate the author's vocabulary and writing style, the main topics, and the pattern of organization of the text. Scan one or two pages in every chapter or the whole article for important words. My favorite way to read trigger words is to scan the index. Sometimes trigger-word reading alone will satisfy your purpose questions. If so, you are finished. For details, pinpoint your purpose and begin PhotoReading.

3. PhotoRead: PhotoReading allows your more-than-conscious mind to "mentally photograph" the printed pages at a speed and depth far beyond the capacity of your conscious mind. You enhance the process by clearly stating your purpose and getting into the accelerated learning state. PhotoRead by making two or more passes through the text, turning pages rhythmically before defocused eyes while chanting to yourself. Afterward, affirm that you have what you need to activate. The complete step may take 10 to 15 minutes, depending on the size of the book.

　• When you are ready to PhotoRead, choose a place where you can concentrate, or choose to concentrate wherever you are. Relax into a frame of mind that allows you to focus within. Prepare your

See the number *Three* and physically relax. Let your body melt into a resting position. Progressively relax your whole body, beginning at the top of your head and moving any tension down and out the tips of your fingers and the tips of your toes.

Think the number *Two* and mentally relax. Float the buzz and clatter of the Beta world right out of your awareness, letting the space of your mind open. Even with your eyes closed, experience your peripheral vision as boundless.

Enter the Accelerated Learning State: Feel the number *One* and imagine a beautiful plant or flower or scene in nature. Then enter your beautiful scene—a place of quiet, comfort, and joy—and experience it vividly. Feel the good feelings here and memorize them. Imagine yourself in an environment complete with pleasant sights you see, sounds you hear, and feelings you feel. Bring forward from your past any resources that spontaneously occur to you to complete your daydream.

If you now gently think about the crown of your head, you will find that your eyes feel as if they are moving slightly apart. This open-minded movement gives a wide peripheral view of the world. Try it. Open your eyes and experiment with focusing on something close, then shifting your attention to the top back part of your head. Notice how your visual range expands before your eyes. In essence, moving to the Alpha state and widening your eyes gives you an instantaneously available new perspective on the world.

mind and body with your favorite relaxation technique.

The technique on the opposite page synchronizes your brain hemispheres and balances and stabilizes your concentration. After the prepare step becomes a habit, you can compress it into a brief progressive relaxation, a glimpse of your beautiful scene, and an affirmation that you are confidently beginning your reading. Prepare precedes the other Whole Mind Reading steps, as well as challenges elsewhere in life.

• To PhotoRead, use PhotoFocus, a relaxed way of seeing with peripheral vision that puts the text directly into the more-than-conscious mind. Prop the text in front of you at a 45 degree angle from the table, or a 90 degree angle from your eyes. Stare above it or "through it" as if you were daydreaming, gazing into space, or resolving random-dot stereograms.

> Fred determines misspellings graphically. "I don't have to read; I just scan, and the wrong words jump off the page because they don't look right."

• Begin PhotoReading by turning the pages at a comfortable speed. In his book *The Gift of Dyslexia*, Ron Davis reports that the more-than-conscious mind seems to absorb UP to 35 frames a second, which you can only reach by fanning pages. Scrolling text on your computer screen will someday provide that speed. Focus at least a yard away and move the text UP into view. For this step, expect the page to look slightly blurry. You may notice that using stereo focus makes looking at the pages as restful as daydreaming. It relaxes the body as well as the eyes. You may notice a slender phantom column appear in the gutter between the two pages, a "blip page," created by binocular vision.

• Begin turning pages rhythmically, about a page a second. Simultaneously, chant to yourself:

Re-lax...Re-lax...
Four-Three-Two-One...
Re-lax...Relax...
Keep the state...See the page...

My favorite chant is "Twinkle, twinkle, little star." If you have specific micro-questions, begin chanting them in a steady rhythm to your page-turning. If you have privacy, chant them aloud; if not, ask them to yourself as you turn the pages rhythmically. If you have existential macro-questions, simply hold them in your mind or state them, as

The integration of visual information is a process in which perception and comprehension of the visible world occur simultaneously.
Semir Zeki
"The Visual Image in Mind and Brain"
Scientific American, September, 1992

Perfectionism is a perfect way to procrastinate.
Charlotte Ward

you choose, and turn the pages rhythmically. A musically inclined friend flips her pages to the undulating rhythms of a Bach cantata in her mind's ear. Intoning words keeps your left brain busy while your right brain absorbs the message.

I usually PhotoRead round trip-once from front to back, and once upside-down and backward from back to front. If I find the subject matter complex, I PhotoRead until I feel satisfied, an accurate albeit subjective indication.

• To complete PhotoReading, affirm that the information you have PhotoRead is within you now and available to you when you want it on a conscious level. You have introduced the ideas to your more-than-conscious mind through non-conscious channels; therefore, the answers you seek may bubble UP spontaneously in dreams or sudden realizations. If you want to bring specific material to consciousness, for instance, find the answer to a question, the next step, Activate, outlines several successful strategies. Ideally, allow the information to incubate overnight or longer, yet many people who PhotoRead, activate immediately with great success.

PhotoReading Instructor and neurophysiologist, Izzy Katzef, MD, suffered a stroke, which partially paralyzed his right side and obliterated a fourth of his visual field, thereby, annihilating his ability to comprehend any written material. After recovering from the trauma, he began playing with PhotoReading again. To his amazement, what he PhotoRead, he could then read with complete conscious comprehension. This was nothing short of a miracle to him. He has hypothesized that PhotoReading sends information directly into the brain via the right hemisphere. Subsequently, researchers have found what may be a neural pathway for visual information that had previously not been known.

4. ACTIVATE: Bring the information to consciousness by any creative expression, including discussing, writing, speaking, dancing, composing music, and drawing.

For activating nonfiction in the business environment, and for fiction, we use super reading and dipping. Always state to yourself your purpose or goal for reading this text. What do you want to know? Do you want to answer macro- or micro-questions? Start with the most inclusive question (See Chapter 10). Turn to the part of the text most aligned with your questions. Then, skim your eyes vertically down the center of the page, following the trail of what you want to Identify, slowly enough to catch trigger words but faster

Montana could check off two covered receivers and throw to a third man, sometimes even finding a way to get the ball to a covered receiver, in part because he didn't have to reflect on the situation at the time.... To introduce conscious decision-making into the process would wreck his timing. As Montana remarked, "If I ever stopped to think about what happens, after the ball hits my hands, it might screw up the whole process."

Timothy Ferris

The Mind's Sky: Human Intelligence in a Cosmic Context

than you can read. When you feel a rush of interest indicating you are close to an answer, regular read the paragraph or so that contains the macro-idea (concept) or micro-idea (detail) you want until you get an *aha*. Record the answer on your pictograph adjacent to the matching question.

George was learning to PhotoRead. Midway through his first book, flip, flip, flip, he turned the pages to the rhythm of a silent chant. A few pages in, he "felt a sharp sensation too painful to ignore, as if I'd stepped on a tack," and the word *banana* popped into his mind. "Hummm," he wondered. Flip, flip, flip, he continued turning pages. Then he went directly to the index, knowing full well there was no such listing as *banana*. Yes, he got no *banana*, but next to where it might have been, there was the word *Blacks*. George was curious, so he found the page. As an African American, he strongly disagreed with an idea there. Surprised, George realized that his right brain had communicated a strong emotional reaction during PhotoReading. He had thought the idea was—*BANANAS*!

• Resume super reading until you sense you have another answer, read a paragraph or so for that answer, and pictograph it around the appropriate question. Your pictograph serves as a trigger to stimulate awareness of what the unconscious mind has stored. Pictograph *aha's* until you have satisfied your initial questions. By answering your macro-questions first, and continuing down the hierarchy until you have answered your micro-questions, you can use your time efficiently. By answering macro-questions first and moving toward micro-questions, you may reach the conscious understanding you desire before you Identify the last of your questions. Stop looking for answers at any time you feel complete.

If you have generated other questions, add those to your pictograph and Identify the answers. You have finished activating when you have answered your questions and, therefore, feel finished.

5. RAPID READ: Begin at the beginning of the text and read at varying speeds to the end, much as if you were driving across town; sometimes you would hit green lights and flow with traffic; sometimes you would slow and sometimes stop before moving on. Remember to state your revised purpose and prepare by going into the Alpha state. Use this last step for the satisfaction of conscious reading, the feeling of "knowing you know" complex material, or to relish the

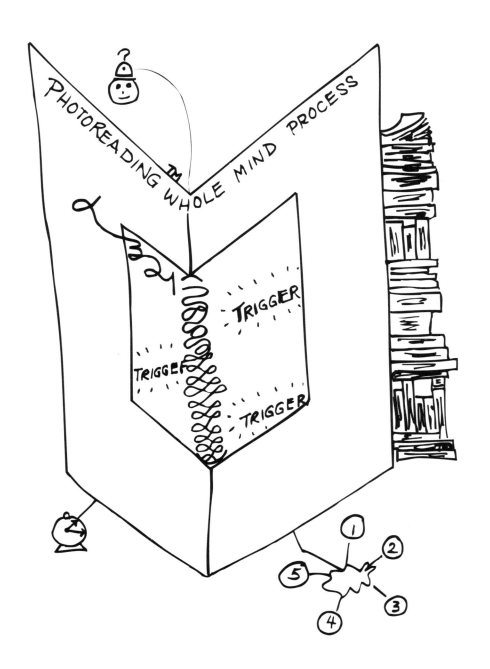

SIMPLY LIVE IT UP

words. I find that I almost never need this step to gather facts or ideas from nonfiction. Rapid reading does, however, offer an overall view of a text and confirmation that you have "read" fiction, but do not be surprised if you fly through the material. After having PhotoRead and activated, you will probably happily discover that the ideas seem too familiar to linger, so you will probably zip along.

Of course, you may find an occasional text that warrants repeated careful reading, in which case, you still and always have your regular reading skills in place for that eventuality.

BRIEF SOLUTION for Chapter 11: The PhotoReading Whole Mind System

STEPS
1. Prepare
2. Preview
3. PhotoRead
4. Activate
5. Rapid Read

ACTION

How do I intend to apply this solution to my life to get the results I want?

What Next Action Step do I plan to take?

The PhotoReading Whole mind system taps into multiple levels of awareness: Beta, Alpha, Theta, and Delta. Our exploration into the Self would be incomplete without investigating that inner space of nighttime wonder, where visions of sugar plums dance in your head, where the wild things are. Open your wonder windows wide as you dream with us in Chapter 12, **Rem Realm**.

SIMPLY LIVE IT UP

CHAPTER 12
REM REALM

*Enlightenment consists
not merely in seeing luminous shapes and visions,
but in making the darkness visible.*
Carl Jung

We have been called from play and from dreaming.
Hugh Downs
Potential: The Way to Emotional Maturity

The more important the message of the dream,
the more intense will be the reaction of the dreamer....
A dream has a purpose, it tells a story,
shows you pictures, and creates emotion.
[A dream] is the self talking to the self.
Phoebe McDonald
Dreams: Night Language of the Soul

Perhaps we have misinterpreted the nature of our lives anyway. When we look at trees we think those unseen, toiling roots and tendrils are there merely to support the flourishing leaves and branches and blossoms. But perhaps the true life of the tree is underground. Is it possible that in our lives we are awake merely to provide material for the essential business of living—sleep and dreams and those long hours when we sink back into the deepest centers of existence?
T. Alan Broughton
"Your Dreams Are Models"
The Writer's Handbook, 1995

CHAPTER 12

REM REALM

PROBLEM

Sometimes I have nightmares.
I dream the same dream repeatedly.
I never dream, at least I don't remember my dreams.
I feel uneasy, as if I were missing out on some secret.
I wish I were more creative.
I'm too tired to dream. The alarm clock jars me awake. I hit the snooze
button several times. Then I finally have to get out of bed. I rarely get
to lie abed in the morning. Who has time to dream?

> *The tremulous earth quivers gently at around ten hertz.*
> *So, in our deepest sleep, we enter synchrony with the trembling*
> *earth. Dreaming, we become the Earth's dream.*
>
> Diane Ackerman
> *The Natural History of the Senses*

WHAT IF . . . ?

- I trusted my dreams as part of my own wisdom
- I planned my day to ensure myself adequate sleep time, so
  that I allowed for rapid-eye-movement -(REM) sleep cycles
  and awakened naturally
- I told myself I could remember my dreams.
- I gave my imagination free rein to flesh out my dreams
- I recorded my dreams in my NightLights while I remained
  in a dreamy state
- I reviewed my dream themes to notice what lessons my
  more-than-conscious mind had sent me
- I programmed myself to participate in my dreams

THEN . . .

I could enjoy "listening" to my own stories from my more-
than-conscious mind. They could light the way for my intuition and
creativity. In the early hours, I could ease back the veil to reveal my
inner Self. Because my more-than-conscious mind studies real life, I

Childhood dreams prompt a journey of self-discovery.
Author Unknown

This dream came to me during a graduate program in counseling when I was reviewing what I had done with my life and wondering what I was going to do:

I am walking down a stone pathway rather like a jetty surrounded on all sides by thick, grey fog. I am accompanied by a guide, whom I cannot see. As we walk, my guide explains that the path is the space between what has been and what will be. To the left is my past. When I look in that direction, the fog lifts, revealing a landscape of meadows, hills, and valleys dotted with houses and connecting roads. To the right is my future, that which may be. As I look, the fog shifts and moves over almost recognizable shapes. My guide tells me that I have the power to make of my future what I will. For a moment it takes the shape of enormous dark blue waves, which almost overwhelm me, but I change them into rolling green hills. My guide then leads me down a short spiral flight of stairs to a gift shop full of wonderful objects. My guide tells me that because I am human, I have the power to turn them into anything I want. I play with the gift my guide hands me, turning it first into one thing, then another.

Soon after, I decided to go on for my doctorate.
Debi Hinton

would enjoy the power of using my conscious mind to decipher the messages and decide courses of action in my waking life. I would find it fun to learn from such a personal and subtle teacher.

SIMPLY

Dreams come to everyone during the phase of rapid eye movement about every hour and a half during the entire night as the rest of the body lies immobile. Sleep scientists recognize dream-bearing REM sleep as paramount to physical and mental health. Treat yourself to the natural inner wisdom available in your night dreams and daydreams. We give proven methods for remembering the wisdom of your REM realm.

LIVE IT

Plurk in the REM realm—the safe venue for receiving whole-brain messages and confronting fears. Our nightly *commedia dell'arte* incorporates the day's lessons into long-term memory. So, want a great memory? Dream. You remember best what you "sleep on." Evolution seems to have reserved a special realm—the mentally urgent, physically immobilized Theta dream state—for integrating new information from the Beta and Alpha worlds.

Most people take dreams seriously; we *need* to take dreaming seriously. Using Theta-world symbols, the more-than-conscious mind paints parables of many moods. Ignored, they transmute and recur. Your dreams seem powerfully to represent your inner mind, like messengers come to inform you what the body politic wants and needs. The very act of remembering a dream sets you gently oscillating between Theta and Alpha states; activate UP to Beta without respectfully recording your dream and risk forgetting the delicate reality entirely. People usually express disappointment at losing track of dreams, as if they had lost a gift. Dreams seem to support all parts of the body-mind to act with integrity and clarity.

Make time to dream. Depriving yourself of sleep, particularly REM sleep, endangers your health. If the body misses its five-or-so dream cycles one night, it dreams more the next—as if body chemistry demands a time-share of each state. If you want health, you need to live in harmony with your ultradian (daily) rhythms, both day and night, which occur naturally in 90-minute cycles.

Some people participate in their dreams as if they were awake. You can learn to lucid dream. As a mammal, you must dream; as a human, you can experiment. What's your pleasure?

Horatio *O day and night, but this is wondrous*
strange!
Hamlet *And therefore as a stranger give it welcome.*
There are more things in heaven and earth,
Horatio,
Than are dreamt of in your philosophy.
William Shakespeare
Hamlet

Consciousness confers the same advantages on the dream state as it does on the waking state. As a consequence, while awake in your dreams you are in a unique position to respond creatively to the unexpected situations you can encounter there. This quality of flexible control, which is characteristic of lucid dreams, brings within reach a remarkable range of possibilities—from indulging your boldest fantasies to fulfilling your highest spiritual aspirations.
Stephen LaBerge
Lucid Dreaming:
The Power of Being Awake and Aware in Your Dreams

SIMPLY LIVE IT UP

UP

If we respect dream messages, we can channel the vitality of our nights into creative days and solve our greatest paradoxes with our eyes closed. The dreaming brain keeps our best and highest purposes in mind. Support peak mental and physical health—dream the wisdom of the information-gatherer to the glory of the egotistic neocortex. As spinners of tall tales and metaphors of most profound import, with your dreams you rival Aesop and Shakespeare. A flexible dramatist, you continue producing scenarios until your protean actors drive their intentions home. Integrating your DayLights and NightLights can give you delight and congruence.

BRIEF SOLUTIONS

1. DayLights

As part of your bedtime routine, reflect on your day: your questions, what inspired you, what things you loved doing, what synchronicities you noticed, what insights bubbled UP, which important people you connected with, anything mystical that happened? Note them on your DayLights on the following page.

While you drift to sleep, review your day to identify what happened of value and what you learned. Macro-perspective of the events and thoughts of the day sets the stage for deciding what you want to dream. Ask questions to elicit dream answers: *What information can manifest to me about...that I can have for my highest good and the highest good of all others concerned?*

2. NightLights

Whenever you think about sleep or dreams, give yourself the suggestion: *I remember my dreams when I awake.* Place within reach by your bed so that you can stay gently in state: pen or pencil, paper, a small night light; or, if you prefer, a tape recorder. If you share quarters with someone, you will need to accommodate his or her sleeping habits. Ideally, retire early enough that you can enjoy two periods of REM sleep close to consciousness at dawn. Give yourself time to dream.

As you dream, surface just enough to tape record or pictograph snippets in your NightLights, all the while maintaining your quiet state. Recount to yourself as many details as you remember. Vivify them to paint them indelibly on your mental palette. While still in state, review your dream, letting your mind follow your pen as you fluidly record what you see, hear, and feel in present tense.

DAYLIGHTS©

MYSTICAL HAPPENINGS

WHAT INSPIRES ME

IMPORTANT PEOPLE

THINGS I LOVE TO DO

BODY NOTES

SYNCHRONICITIES

INSIGHTS

NIGHTLIGHTS

DREAM DIRECTIVES: What questions do I want to dream on?

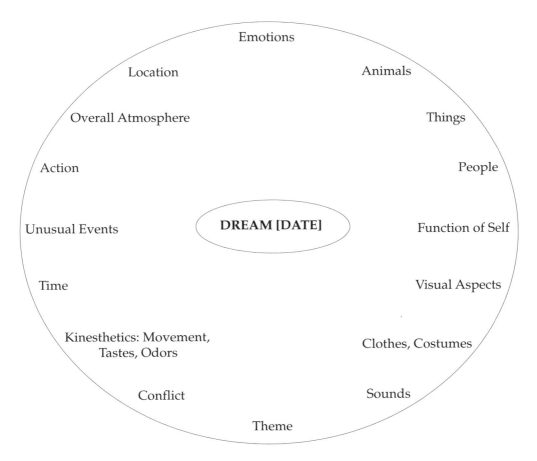

HIGHLIGHTS: What does my dream mean? *(Write an aphorism expressing the MORAL, LESSON, OR CREATIVE IDEA?)*
Elevate each specific dream element to a higher perspective; e.g.,
house = life; road = choices; garbage= abundance

3. HighLights

As you gently come to the Alpha state, actively wonder what the dream means. Let your imagination rove freely over various interpretations. Consider playfully and open-mindedly your dream symbols. Mentally transpose each dream element from the status of a detail to the status of a symbol. Play with the subtleties. Expect a spontaneous sensation of *aha* when you hit upon the meaning of the symbol and perhaps a distinct feeling of physical-mental Integration. Write down the message of the dream—the HighLight—so that your conscious mind can see it, read it, and "know" it on all levels of your being. Anticipate your day as you connect your plans with the HighLights of the dream.

Review your NightLights frequently for similar stories or themes rising from the Theta side of the conscious veil. Thank your more-than-conscious and conscious minds for their cooperative wisdom in helping you achieve what you want. You can use you dreams as a source for creativity—in music, poetry, dance, visual arts, writing, planning speeches and presentations, learning languages, and much more.

May your fondest dreams come true.

BRIEF SOLUTIONS for Chapter 12

1. DayLights
2. NightLights
3. HighLights

ACTION

How do I intend to apply these solutions to my life to get the results I want?

What Next Action Step do I plan to take?

Wake UP! You can also solve paradoxes with your eyes open. Chapter 13 adventures into the paradoxes of life with an intriguing twist of practicality. At this point in the book, you are either ready to give up or give UP—to **Identity and the Infinite I.**

SIMPLY LIVE IT UP

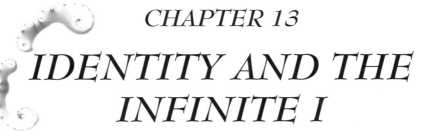

CHAPTER 13
IDENTITY AND THE INFINITE I

To light a candle is to cast a shadow....
Ursula LeGuin
A Wizard of Earthsea

*People will travel a long way to see a "view."
The essential element of a good view is distance, and
preferably with nothing human in the immediate fore-
ground. When we stand on a hill and look across fifty
miles of emptiness at the mountains, we are experiencing the pleasure of having our space flow out un-
hindered. As people come in sight of a view, it's nor-
mal for their posture to improve and for them to breathe
better. You can see people remarking on the freshness
of the air, and taking deep breaths, although it's the
same air as it was just below the brow of the hill. Trips
to the sea, and our admiration of mountains are probably symptoms of overcrowding.*

Keith Johnstone
Impro: Improvisation and the Theatre

Walk the mystical path with practical feet.

Angeles Arrien
The Four-Fold Way

SIMPLY LIVE IT UP

CHAPTER 13

IDENTITY AND THE INFINITE I

PROBLEM

I know I am part of the whole, yet I lose sight of who I am.
I sometimes feel depressed, jealous, confused, or lonely.
I have a tough time making important choices.
I don't know when to use a system (create my reality) and when to let go (be available for what happens in the moment).
Once I commit to something, I feel I should not back out.

> *Attain an attitude of altitude.*
> George Emery

WHAT IF . . . ?

- I soared to a bird's-eye view of my life to make choices
- I made choices and commitments in accord with my highest values and purpose
- I recognized and accepted my intrinsic aptitudes
- I interacted positively and flexibly with my environment
- I periodically reassessed and updated my commitments

THEN . . .

I would live my spirituality instead of "doing" it. I would express myself, which would make me feel useful in the world. I would face what naturally came to me, and live mindful of my power to take responsibility for myself and make choices. My commitments would reflect my current values. My systems would support me, not run my life. I would learn from the past without guilt, live in the present with joy, and anticipate the future with confidence.

SIMPLY

This chapter reviews the importance of knowing when to transcend to a macro-perspective and the benefits of doing so. Other

I-WORDS

I
icon
iconoclast
iconoscope
idea
ideal
identity
identify
ideogram
ideograph
ideology
idiosyncrasy
idiom
ignite
illuminate
illustrate
imagine
imbue
impact
impart
impassion
impel
impetus
implement
implicit
impresario
impressionable
improvise
impulse
impute
incentive
incisive
increment
incubate
incur
indeed
indelible
independent
index
indicate
individual
indomitable
induct
industry

ineffable
inestimable
infallible
infant
infer
infinite
inflection
inflorescence
influx
inform
infuse
ingenious
ingenuous
ingrained
ingredient
inhabit
initial
initiate
innervate
innocent
innovation
innumerable
inquire
insatiable
inscribe
inscrutable
insight
insouciant
instance
instant
instate
instill
instinct
insure
intact
intake
integral
integrate
integrity
intellect
intelligence
intend
intense
intent

intercom
intercourse
interest
interlude
intermission
internal
international
interpolate
interplay
interpolate
interpose
interpret
interracial
interrogation
intersect
intersperse
interstice
interval
interview
intimate
intricate
introduce
introspection
intuition
invaluable
invent
investigate
invigorate
invincible
invisible
invite
invoke
involute
involve
invulnerable
ion
IQ
irrational
irrelevant
irrepressible
irresistible
ism
issue
iterate

chapters address how to create systems for ease and effectiveness of living. You may find it equally useful to know how to and when to let go of those systems.

These age-old questions still puzzle the philosopher in us:

- Who am I? *Who* am I? Who *am* I? Who am *I*?
- Where do I fit into the universe?
- What ideals do I aspire to? What beliefs do I hold? What things do I value?
- What intrinsic talents make me capable of contributing?
- What shall I do?
- How shall I interact with others, things, and situations?

This chapter identifies ten of life's paradoxes alongside playful and thoughtful exercises for you to discover your Identify and the Infinite I behind your actions and beliefs.

LIVE IT

Walter, two years from retirement, values an adequate retirement income. He owns two properties that provide rental income, rapid turnover, and a lot of maintenance. He dreads the maintenance, but he must do it himself to make the venture cost-effective. He also dislikes interviewing potential tenants. He loses sleep and feels edgy at work. He even finds it difficult to have fun because he worries about his property.

Taking care of the property disturbs his inner peace. He chooses to act in harmony with his highest values. By selling the two properties, he regains inner peace and creatively looks at other ways to earn money for retirement security.

Moving to a macro position increases your flexibility so you can access flow. Naming brings focus. Notice whether what you say defines you, limits you, or frees you. If you know who you are and what you want, you can decide to act purposefully and expect sureness, congruence, efficiency, effectiveness, spirituality, and joy.

UP

All of this chapter touches on UPliftment—acclivous thinking, high perspectives, broad vistas, and encompassing viewpoints—giving UP to the Infinite I. Giving UP is a paradox. It may seem like losing, but remember when you played hide-and-seek? Remember the fun when you allowed your friends to find you? Giving UP can

There's no better exercise
for strengthening the heart than reaching down
and lifting people up.
Author Unknown

Balancing the opposites, or switching between them,
must not be a random or haphazard act....
The secret of balance in a time of paradox
is to allow the past and the future to coexist
in the present.
Jack Schwarz
Voluntary Controls: Exercises for Creative Meditation

Paradox: (from Gr. para *beyond;* doxon *opinion) a*
statement of inconsistent or contradictory elements,
where the elements themselves
seem to be incongruously true

mean letting go of one level of control to participate at a higher level.

Giving UP can also mean to be of service. Everyone can serve because service takes many shapes and forms. Being the best you can be serves you and others.

> Returning home from a business trip, I discovered on boarding the bus that I had only a twenty-dollar bill but not the required exact change. As I turned around with a hapless expression, ready to get off, I found myself face to face with a street person, who asked if I needed something. I stumbled over my words, being honest about my situation. Graciously he handed me the money. I asked for his address to return what I perceived I was borrowing, only to remember he was homeless. He smiled, "I like to help, too." His sincerity made it clear that I could accept without feeling guilty. I "gave up" to his generosity.

What puzzles you on one level may come clear with perspective. Acting at your highest levels can being peace and power, as well as all your best attributes on lower levels. Paradoxically, when you surrender to wisdom, you gain control over yourself. At the core of what you do lives your essence—the Self at one with the Infinite—the Infinite I encompasses the identity with Oneness.

Infinite
I
Ideals
Intrinsics
Initiatives
Interactions

BRIEF SOLUTIONS

Paradox: Everyone is eccentric. To know ourselves, we must not only go within to assess our visions, thoughts, and feelings but also, in the opposite direction, to take "objective" and varied points of view outside ourselves.

1. Who Am I? First, draw a representation of you in the center of a

Pat yourself all over saying, "This is I.
This body belongs to me."
Ron Klein

We don't see things as they are,
we see them as we are.
Anais Nin

Lights of the round table
Phil Nelson

...this ambiguous earth....
Alice Meynell

All views of the world are required...
Mary Catherine Bateson
Peripheral Visions: Learning Along the Way

SIMPLY LIVE IT UP

page. Begin pictographing your Identity from the standpoint of Interactions: from the viewpoint of a close friend, then through the eyes of a stranger, and from the community perspective. Next, pictograph your Initiatives—the things you do in the world, followed by your Intrinsics—what things you can do, your capabilities, whether or not you now do them. Then pictograph your Ideals—your values and beliefs. Through your own eyes looking gently at yourself, pictograph your Identity. And lastly, from the Infinite perspective, pictograph yourself in relation to the Infinite I. If you like, take in your pictograph as a hologram. Pat yourself all over, saying, "This is I. This body belongs to me. I choose how I manifest myself in the universe."

Paradox: We can control our feelings; we can control nothing. With an imaginary Circle of Light we can change ourselves and our world.
2. Circle of Light:

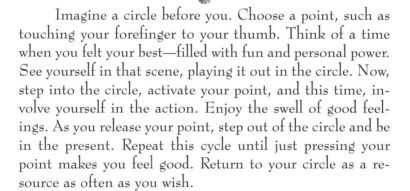

Imagine a circle before you. Choose a point, such as touching your forefinger to your thumb. Think of a time when you felt your best—filled with fun and personal power. See yourself in that scene, playing it out in the circle. Now, step into the circle, activate your point, and this time, involve yourself in the action. Enjoy the swell of good feelings. As you release your point, step out of the circle and be in the present. Repeat this cycle until just pressing your point makes you feel good. Return to your circle as a resource as often as you wish.

Paradox: The shortsighted ignore the long view. Hungry is the eagle who preys on the ground.
3. Lift-Off: Sometimes we restrict our results to what we see immediately ahead of us. By lifting ourselves and soaring to the height of our Ideals, we see a different view—a vista. When two values or beliefs appear to be in conflict, consider them from above, from the transcendent vantage point of your Identity and the Infinite I.

Paradox: We know what fulfills us, yet we do not know exactly how we know.

Until you are at home somewhere,
you cannot be at home everywhere.
Mary Catherine Bateson
Peripheral Visions: Learning Along the Way

Without a belief in human unity,
I am hungry and incomplete....
Human unity is...the harmony of opposites.
Norman Cousins
The Celebration of Life:
A Dialogue on Immortality and Infinity

Sometimes in our endeavor to sit back and wait to
hear what the universe has to say, we forget that we
are the center of our universe.
Vicky Coates, Stellenbach, South Africa

SIMPLY LIVE IT UP

4. What Fulfills Me: In the center of a piece of paper using colors, draw a star with many-colored rays emanating from it. In the center of the star, write "What Fulfills Me." At the end of each ray, pictograph something that fulfills you. Use few words.

Paradox: The more heated the interchange, the greater the profit from macro-perspective, playfulness, and open-mindedness.
5. 29: When you feel yourself reacting to what others say and do in an emotional confrontation, practice the pause. Before you answer, list 29 ways you might respond, starting with the silliest. Play out at least three scenarios in your imagination. Chose the one that benefits all. Credit yourself for your measured judgment.

Paradox: What we did yesterday has passed, yet it forms our today. As we move through the day, we may not consider many of the things we do as purposeful, yet on reflection, we can see the framework of our choices. Change yesterday's frame, change the choices of tomorrow: power where you may not have recognized power before.
6. Yesterday: Name four actions you took yesterday. Identify what values and beliefs underlay those actions.

Paradox: "Sticks and stones can break my bones, but words can never hurt me"; but "You get what you say."
7. What's in a Name?: For *selfish*, substitute *centered* or *self-caring*.

Paradox: Most of the brain works wordlessly yet mindfully.
8. To Be or Not To Be: Use To-Be verbs—am, is, are, was, were, have been, had been, etc., specifically to express Identity, not feelings and actions. "I am sad" and "I feel sad" mean different things. The "body electric" turns on to the deep meaning of your words.

Paradox: We want conscious control, yet we would never want to have to control everything. In fact, we resist change because we must use consciousness instead of autopilot as we develop a new habit.
9. Back-Seat Driver: Verbally instruct yourself to walk upstairs, including how to balance and which muscles to contract and which to lengthen in the precise sequence. Good luck.

Paradox: To feel alone, simply close the eyes; to feel connected with the universe, simply close the eyes. We separate; we join. There is no aloneness; there is no togetherness. Both-And: Alone-Together.
10. One: Turn the light of your consciousness on how much time you like to spend alone and how much doing things with others.

IDentity AND THE INFINITE IS

VALUE
VALUE
VALUE
VALUE
VALUE

PARADOX PARADOX
PARADOX PARADOX

To rest and clear the mind, repeat the word *One* to yourself, and gently close your eyes. See the blank space behind your closed lids. Note the limits of your field of vision and sense of mind. Think *One* in slow rhythm with your pulse. Breathing fully, continue thinking *One* as you widen the aperture of your vision and note the mind's boundary moving outward. Let the inner sound of *One* soften to a whisper, then fade into awareness alone. Sense the mind as hologram—energy without time or mass. Stay in this space as long as you like. To return, focus ever closer with the mind's-eye, take a full breath, and gently open the eyes.

LIST OF BRIEF SOLUTIONS for Chapter 13

1. Who Am I?
2. Circle of Light
3. Lift-Off
4. What Fulfills Me?
5. 29
6. Yesterday
7. What's in a Name?
8. *To Be* or *Not To Be*
9. Back-Seat Driver
10. One

ACTION

How do I intend to apply these solutions to my life to get the results I want?

What Next Action Step do I plan to take?

Transpose yourself to a time filled with receptivity, curiosity, wonder, and creativity. Proceed to Chapter 14, but stay alert. You may end UP going to the beginning to **Simply Live It Up**.

CHAPTER 14
SIMPLY LIVE IT UP

There was a child went forth every day,
And the first object he looked upon,
that object he became,
And that object became part of him
for the day or a certain part of the day,
Or for many years or
stretching cycles of years.

Walt Whitman
"There Was a Child Went Forth"

Rising
with adventurous eyes, feet and spirit
like an eagle's first flight
A veritable
p a n o r a m i c
picnic of puzzle pieces.

Teri-E Belf, Phil Nelson
"Above the Tree Line"

So long we have tried to achieve perfection
when all we have gained is protection
from our innocence.

Kim Allen Williams
"From Innocence to Ignorance"

CHAPTER 14

SIMPLY LIVE IT UP

PROBLEM

I'm stuck.
I never do well on tests.
I'm afraid to try new things.
I panic when people watch me.
I've never done this...before.
I should be perfect.

I'm a lifetime learner.
Art Wilkerson

WHAT IF . . . ?

- I chose receptivity, curiosity, wonder, and creativity as my approach to living
- I responded to the new as an opportunity
- I acted out of a sense of self-esteem and "can-do"
- I concentrated my full attention on the object of interest, instead of on myself
- I gave myself over to the delight of discovery

THEN . . .

I would get results. I would enjoy learning. I would express enthusiasm. I would live in synchrony with change. I would open my life to all kinds of possibilities.

SIMPLY

You can open wide your door to fun, personal power, intuition, and creativity.

LIVE IT

Whenever you accomplish anything, you show that you have made a choice to keep learning. Paradoxically, your route to knowl-

The timeless attitude. Focusing on the moment and shedding the past and future. This does not, of course, mean abolishing memory (past) or anticipation and planning (future).... A timeless attitude toward the "now" makes the past exist only in memory and the future no more than a vast number of possibilities with varying probabilities—both past and future being useful, but not real in the sense that life at the present moment is real.

Hugh Downs
Potential: The Way to Emotional Maturity

My memory is personal and finite,
but my substance is boundless and infinite.
Norman Cousins
The Celebration of Life:
A Dialogue on Immortality and Infinity

edge took you into uncharted territory. For that time, you turned your back on the false security of being an expert to enter the attitude of the child-mind. You freed yourself UP to learn. To take an exam or face any other immediate challenge or glitch, shift from a stultifying self-conscious loop to an invigorating fascination with something beyond. Whenever you direct your attention to what you want to know, you will discern patterns of the universe.

UP

You have a birthright—an invitation to greatness—a potential for mastery. Masters enter a situation expecting to discover something. They welcome UPdates. They search out the new. Masters get emotional and spiritual charge from the very act of learning. What you choose to learn expresses your Identity and UPlifts you. In the act of learning, you realize your life purpose.

BRIEF SOLUTION: Enter the Attitude of the Child-Mind

If you feel daunted and fear you will fail and humiliate yourself, follow the UPcoming script. Instead of concentrating on yourself, focus on what you want as you venture forth with this fresh approach to learning. Replace the ball and cat with the idea or thing you desire in a spirit of receptivity, curiosity, wonder, and creativity:

Whenever you grow anxious about performing, quiet your other senses and listen carefully to your inner dialogue. Listen to what you say to yourself in your mind's ear. Listen to the voices telling you what to do and the voices expressing judgments about you; listen to the voices telling you how they would have done things and how you should do this and not that. Listen to the voices, one at a time. Identify who is speaking to you. Then, host a party for voices; introduce them. As soon as they begin talking to each other and pay you no mind, ease yourself a little distance away.

The more they talk, let the sweeter grow their harmonies. Let each part evolve into a color, and listen to the tune as the colors spin and whirl round and round. As you move farther still, see the colors spin into a ball spinning farther

Admire the world for never ending on you—
as you would admire an opponent,
without taking your eyes from him,
or walking away.
Annie Dillard
The Writing Life

Curiosity is a stronger force than gravity.
If it weren't, there wouldn't be airplanes.
Curiosity is more important than knowledge;
it is the root of knowledge. Without it
there wouldn't be any such thing as knowledge.
Most importantly, curiosity is the dynamic force
behind creativity.
Without creativity, [human]kind
would still be living in caves.
Ronald D. Davis
The Gift of Dyslexia

and farther away from you. When you no longer see the colors or hear their music, close your eyes and relax. Let your mind still. As your space quiets, bask in the sound of silence. *State of Being*

In this silence, imagine being a young child or a baby once again. Look around at the world through wide eyes. *State of Receptivity*

Almost everywhere you look interests you, invites you. Exciting possibilities appear in all directions. You approach everything as a toy. *State of Curiosity*

Bypassing things you recognize, you explore interesting things you find in your path. What's that? You reach for the new. Ouch! You cry. Just then, you spot something else farther on, something you have never seen before. You let out a squeal of glee and head for it. Plopping down in front of it, you stretch your fingers for the many-colored shape, when you touch it, it rolls out of reach.

You move closer and reach again. This time you stretch far enough beyond it to stop it. You concentrate on grasping it. Yes! As you do, it makes a chiming sound. Oh! You squeeze it. It sounds again. The longer you squeeze, the more notes sound. You squeeze out music. When you stop squeezing, it stops sounding. You pat it, expecting part of a tune you heard before. The little bells tinkle. They sound funny. You laugh. *State of Wonder*

You pat it-pat, pat, pat. It sings, sings, sings. You scoop it off the floor and follow it with your eyes, above your head. It rolls on your open palm, off the tips of your fingers, whirling through the air, landing with a quick ring, and rolls, rolls, rolls the colors away.

On track again, you race on all fours toward the pretty rolling sound, when the family cat catches your eye. Her tail stands straight UP, fluffed and tricolored. You remember having touched the silky coat. The fascination of moments ago lies where it rolled—its lesson over for today, its time to come again, or not. But, the cat, ah, the cat. She

Push it. Examine all things intensely
and relentlessly.... Do not leave it,
do not course over it, as if it were understood,
but instead follow it down until you see it
in the mystery of its own specificity and strength.
Annie Dillard
The Writing Life

If you combine the eyes of a child
with the attention span of an adult,
you get an artist.
John I. Smith

What is essential is to realize that
children learn independently, not in bunches;
that they learn out of interest and curiosity,
not to please or appease the adults in power;
and that they ought to be in control of
their own learning, deciding for themselves
what they want to learn
and how they want to learn it.
John Holt
How Children Learn

meows, eyeing you through slotted green eyes, and noise-lessly skirts your reach. Your hands work in anticipation. You pat them together, imitating the *meow* Brother makes when he pets the cat. But, wise to your antics, she swishes around the corner and disappears.

You follow her with your gaze, which inadvertently lights on Mommy. Homeward bound for cuddling and food. In your morning nap during long periods of rapid-eye-move-ment sleep, you retrace your waking route, cataloging the nuances of your learning spree.

At no time do you make a mistake. At no time can anyone force you to learn something you don't want to. At no time do you have to linger on a lesson you have already processed. You intake information at your own rate. You automatically seek the stimulations you need. You stop when you finish. You act entirely in a state of personal power: delight, play, wonder, flow, and unselfconscious absorption to discover for yourself the way your world works. Basking in the security of your mother's omnipresence, you search out the new and the different. Unselfconsciously, you exist and act with mastery. You learn as a impulsive passion.

Dear One, you delight in knowing where you are go-ing, yet you love surprises—games, stories, making noise, and moving to where things are happening. You put no bar-rier between yourself and others, reaching to be picked up, cuddled, and kissed. You dream much of the time you sleep, and you sleep a lot. You respond intuitively, eager for trial and giving up error quickly. If you cry when it hurts, almost immediately you open up with a squeal to another possibil-ity. Naturally determined and self-motivated, you observe and imitate—the same way you build a block castle—on the foundation of previous knowledge. *State of Creativity*

You are the hope of our future.

BRIEF SOLUTION for Chapter 15: Attitude of the Child-Mind

STEPS

1. Identify something you want to learn
2. For now, suspend fear, sadness, anger, and need for perfection
3. Close your eyes, relax, still the mind. Engage *Being*
4. Shift into the attitude of the child-mind, breathe, and look around you with new eyes. Engage *Receptivity*
5. In your imagination, from the child-mind perspective, "happen upon" the idea or thing you want to learn. Engage *Curiosity*
6. Investigate it as you might a toy, and allow your mind to fill with questions about it. Engage *Wonder*
7. See, hear, touch, taste, smell, and feel until you have had "enough" for this session. You may want to re-investigate and inquire into the nature of the idea or thing at a later time
8. Dream to integrate your learning. Engage *Creativity*
9. Venture forth into the world to apply what you have learned

ACTION

How do I intend to apply this Brief Solution to my life to get the results I want?

What Next Action Step do I plan to take?

After turning your glitches to your advancement, envisioning your compelling future, lighting your inner fire, ordering your schedule, your belongings, and your associates for your well-being, after adopting a Plurkful attitude, sharpening your wits, and incorporating your dreams as a source of inner wisdom, after taking stock of who you are and what results you want, we hope you will join us as we purposefully engage receptivity, curiosity, Oneder, and creativity to SIMPLY LIVE IT UP!

BIBLIOGRAPHY

Davis, Ron, with Eldon M. Braun. *The Gift of Dyslexia: Why Some of the Smartest People Can't Read and How They Can Learn.* Burlingame, CA: Ability Workshop, 1994.

Dement, M.D. William C. *The Sleepwatchers.* Palo Alto, CA: Stanford Alumni Association, 1992.

Ferris, Timothy. *The Mind's Sky: Human Intelligence in a Cosmic Context.* New York: Bantam, 1992.

Grudin, Robert. *The Grace of Great Things: Creativity and Innovation.* New York: Ticknor and Fields, 1990.

Hobson, J. Allan. *The Dreaming Brain: How the Brain Creates Both the Sense and the Nonsense of Dreams.* New York: Basic-HarperCollins, 1988.

Kline, Peter. *The Everyday Genius: Restoring Children's Natural Joy of Living—and Yours Too.* Arlington, VA: Great Ocean, 1988.

Lakein, Alan. *How To Get Control of Your Time and Your Life.* New York: New American, 1973.

LaBerge, Stephen. *Lucid Dreaming.* Los Angeles: Tarcher, 1985.

Nadeau, Robert L. *Mind, Machines, and Human Consciousness: Are There Limits to Artificial Intelligence?* Chicago: Contemporary, 1991.

Restak, M.D., Richard M. *The Modular Brain: How New Discoveries in Neuroscience are answering Age-Old Questions about Memory, Free Will, Consciousness, and Personal Identity.* New York: Scribner's, 1994.

Rose, Colin. *Accelerated Learning.* New York: Dell, 1985.

Rossi, Ernest, with David Nimmons. *The Twenty-Minute Break: Using the New Science of Ultradian Rhythms.* Los Angeles: Tarcher, 1991.

Scheele, Paul R. *The PhotoReading Whole Mind System.* Wayzata, MN: Learning Strategies Corporation, 1993.

Schwarz, Jack. *Voluntary Controls*. New York: Dutton, 1978; Penguin, 1992.

Stephan, Naomi. *Finding Your Life Mission: How To Unleash that Creative Power and Live with Intention*. Walpole, NH: Stillpoint, 1989.

---. *Fulfill Your Soul's Purpose*: *Ten Creative Paths to Your Life Mission*. Walpole, NH: Stillpoint, 1994.

Thurston, Mark. *Discovering Your Soul's Purpose*. Virginia Beach, VA: A.R.E., 1984.

--- and Christopher Fazel. *The Edgar Cayce Handbook for Creating Your Future*. NY: Ballantine, 1992.

Wonder, Jacquelyn, and Priscilla Donovan. *Whole-Brain Thinking: Working with Both Sides of the Brain To Achieve Peak Job Performance*. New York: Morrow, 1984.

Zink, Nelson. *The Structure of Delight*. Taos, NM: Mind Matters, 1991.

INDEX

ABOUT THE AUTHORS

Teri-E Belf, M.A., C.A.G.S., coaches clients in productivity, life planning, and spirituality, heartens audiences with her public speaking, publishes articles, and facilitates group seminars and retreats. As the Founder of Success Unlimited Network (SUN)®, she coordinates Success Coaches across the United States and directs the national SUN Network. She draws upon a B.A. in psychology from Oberlin College, and two advanced degrees in Education Research and Evaluation. Her 25-years' experience spans management, training, human resources, life planning, and productivity. Teri-E's purpose in life is to inspire and guide people to take steps toward their dreams. She enthusiastically displays purposeful living everyday. She has a son, Kim, and she lives with her husband, Phil, in Fairfax County, Virginia.

For information about these programs, and how to contact the nearest certified Success Coach, call or fax Teri-E Belf at 703 941-3148.

The Success Coaching Program[©]
Consult with a personal Success Coach over six months to help you design your destiny and achieve the results you want in all areas of your life with well-being, satisfaction, and fulfillment. An inspiring, fun, successful program.

SUN Certification Program
Become certified to use the unique and practical coaching techniques: The Results Game, The Well-Being Game, and Guidelines for Winning, to help your personal and business clients achieve results and well-being.

Other Programs

The Personal Productivity Program[©], **The Recareering Program**[©], **The Office Productivity Program, A Purposeful Day**[©]**, Delve Deeper into Your Spirituality Retreat**[©]

Charlotte Ward, M.A., leads seminars, writes and edits books, consults and speaks. Since 1992 Charlotte has been teaching The PhotoReading whole mind system in private sessions and open seminars. Master Practitioner of Neuro-Linguistic Programming, Charlotte has studied and used Ericksonian hypnosis since 1983. She earned a Master's Degree "With Distinction" from Georgetown University and taught high school English accelerated classes in St. Petersburg, Florida. She and Fred Ward have collaborated on four children, who are all pursuing careers in the arts, and on their initial writing project, *The Home Birth Book*. In addition to creating her own poetry and prose, Charlotte has edited numerous works written by her husband. They reside in Bethesda, Maryland. Charlotte has committed her career to facilitating mastery in learning, believing that by opening the window of the mind to ideas from within and from outside, people realize themselves, make beneficial choices, and create rich lives for themselves and others.

For information about **The PhotoReading™Whole Mind System Seminars**, call Charlotte Ward, Accelerated Learning of Maryland, at 301-365-812 or fax 301-983-3980.

What clients say about our Brief Solutions

This has been the best investment of time, money, and emotional feelings I have ever made. Bob Katula, Special Assistant to a Member of Congress

The most important results have been achieving balance and increasing my enjoyment among the different parts of my life. Lee Adamson, Program Marketing Manager, computer industry

This program has an incredible amount to offer at a time when people are lost in this age of demands and choices. Phebe Bowditch, Artist and Teacher

I had been depending on magic, now I can make magic. Candace White, President, Management Support Systems Int'l

I am more confident/validated that there is something inside me worth bringing out and sharing. Carol Havranek, Training Administrator

I have never felt happier, more productive, and directed in my life. Elsie Hui Chang, Political Fund Raiser

I feel more in control. I put down on paper meaningful words I'm feeling. When I lose track of things, I can go back to the words. They're still there. Grace Murphy, Accounting Business Owner

I increased my ability to focus and organize. Dorothy Remy, Ph.D., Anthropologist

I have lost a gnawing doubt that maybe I am not okay. Corrine S. Kills Pretty Enemy, President, First Principles, Inc.

I now can relax about the speed of time and accentuate the being part of my Results Game rather than driven by the task side. Bonnie Kyte, Award-winning Realtor, 100% Club

Guidelines for Winning gave me greater self-awareness to become a lifetime learner. Carrie Norris, Banker-Assistant Vice President

I now have tools to get me out of stuck places and a framework for managing my life from a wholistic perspective. Tina Anderson, Management Consultant, U.S. Army